The Rest of Your Life

Building a House of Sobriety

A Workshop on Alcoholism

By Allen Reid McGinnis

The Rest of Your Life

2nd Edition Published 2010

Copyright © 1986 by J & N Publishing, Oroville, California.

All rights reserved

Printed in the United States of America.

Quotes acknowledged by asterisks are reprinted with permission of Alcoholics Anonymous World Services, Inc. From ALCOHOLICS ANONYMOUS

"Highway Sunset" Photo by Marc Dunn

The Rest of Your Life

Dedication

This book is dedicated to all those who have loved this man for sharing his experience, strength and hope... and to all those who seek and will hopefully find some answers through reading the written words.

The Rest of Your Life

The Rest of Your Life

Contents

Introduction to Second Edition	7
Foreword	9
Session I, July 4, 1968	11
What's the Point of Sobriety?	
Question and Answer Period	
Session 2, July II, 1968	35
Is a Spiritual Experience Necessary?	
Question and Answer Period	
Session 3, July I8, 1968	59
What Are the Old Ideas?	
Question and Answer Period	
Session 4, July 25, 1968	89
The Neurotic Nine!	
Question and Answer Period	
Session 5, August 1, 1968	117
After the Old Ideas, What?	
Question and Answer Period	
San Mateo, Three Years Later	153
Introduction	
Sharing	

The Rest of Your Life

The Rest of Your Life

INTRODUCTION TO THE SECOND EDITION

"I'd like you to think of this, not as a meeting, but as a workshop, where you and I come together and talk about this thing that we share called alcoholism; what I have learned about it, what I have come to believe about it, what you have come to believe about it, and things you might want to know ... questions that are in your mind.

One of the most incredible things about this organization is that I can tell you things that I have come to believe with every fiber of my being, and you can disagree with every syllable I utter, and yet both of us can be sober...both of us can be useful, productive members, not only of Alcoholics Anonymous, but of society. So, if anything I say bothers you, just dismiss it. If anything I say you disagree with, you're entitled to...

Nobody speaks officially for the Fellowship of Alcoholics Anonymous, not even the founders."

Allen Reid McGinnis began his seminars with this disclaimer and repeated a version of it during each "workshop" he conducted. He was a teacher and understood his imperfections and honestly attempted to confront them during his life. He shared what he had "come to believe". He was a person who wanted to be human and most importantly just "be".

We are all on a journey and our searching can be honest, but not perfect. The joyous and free lives we seek come with mistakes and imperfections. The storms we encounter are inevitable, but they are not who we are. We are how we live through the storms.

The Rest of Your Life

The following transcripts of his "workshop" are his answers to the following questions:

1	What's the Point of Sobriety?
2	Is a Spiritual Experience Necessary?
3	What are the Old Ideas?
4	The Neurotic Nine!
5	After the Old Ideas, What?
6	Three Years Later…

Allen's message came to me through a set of circumstances that I believe was a message of how I can be more useful to my fellows; how I can help others break the cycle of neuroses in their families and inspire others to stay sober, "one day at a time".

His words have inspired me to be more useful to the Fellowship and my Community, to chair Big Book Study Groups, to take meetings into Institutions, work on committees, help others through the steps, volunteer for activities at my Place of Worship, and be helpful and thankful to my co-workers and appreciative of my friends outside The Rooms. As it says in Alcoholics Anonymous Step 12; "…to practice these principles in all of my affairs."

It had always been the intent of Mr. McGinnis to help others with this disease.   J & N Publishing was the first to make this message available in print. The purpose of this edition is to share Allen's message, and help as many others as possible.

Thank you J & N Publishing for giving me this opportunity, and Thank God that I was listening.

By Marc Dunn 2010

The Rest of Your Life

Foreword

Allen was a native of Oklahoma, received his education In Catholic parochial schools and attended the University of Tulsa. Before turning to advertising, he had a successful career as a writer of short stories. He also had several plays produced by various civic theatres as well as summer stock companies.

He joined a highly respected advertising firm in 1945 after his discharge from the Army and in the more than twenty years that followed he wrote copy for many large accounts working up to TV writing in the '50s and eventually becoming Creative Director and a Vice-President in the company. His list of advertising awards was long and varied. Allen was a past president of The Copy Club of Los Angeles and a member of the permanent advertising committee for the United Crusade.

This was the public man who entered the Fellowship of Alcoholics Anonymous in 1952. Those of us who were there when he shared his "Workshop on Alcoholism" in 1968 and many who have heard the tapes of those five Thursday night talks over the last

The Rest of Your Life

seventeen years feel that an opportunity was presented to find out what kind of foundation was needed upon which we could build a house of sobriety that would be secure.

The words that have been transcribed and printed onto the following pages have been edited as little as possible ... with many prayers for guidance ... and hopefully will be of benefit to those who have requested they be printed. The question and answer periods have also been included with all names of persons omitted respecting our tradition of anonymity. These further clarify frequently asked questions and contain a degree of humor. The editor only wishes that the many healthy sounds of laughter shared by all, questioners included could have been inserted. If the reader is trudging our road, they will be heard.

A talk that Allen gave in 1971 ... one of the last times he shared ... has also been transcribed and reprinted here. It is possible to learn from it much about how life can happen to us sober when we are challenged to put into practice what we have heard and learned through the years. It isn't always easy, but it is possible if the foundation is solid. Shortly after this talk, and perhaps providing some explanation of how our physical condition can affect our reaction to life situations, Allen was diagnosed as having cancer. He died of that cancer in November of 1972... Sober... and still giving hope and encouragement to those who were there.

The Rest of Your Life

Session 1
July 4, 1968

The Rest of Your Life

What's the point of sobriety?

What's the Point of Sobriety?

I'D LIKE you to think of this, not as a meeting, but as a workshop, where you and I come together and talk about this thing that we share called alcoholism; what I have learned about it, what I have come to believe about it, what you have come to believe about it, and things you might want to know ... questions that are in your mind. Because I saw so many newcomer's hands go up I want to emphasize to you, and don't ever forget it, nobody speaks officially for the Fellowship of Alcoholics Anonymous, not even the founders.

One of the most incredible things about this organization is that I can tell you things that I have come to believe with every fiber of my being, and you can disagree with every syllable I utter, and yet both of us can be sober ... both of us can be

The Rest of Your Life

useful, productive members, not only of Alcoholics Anonymous, but of society. So, if anything I say bothers you, just dismiss it. If anything I say you disagree with, you're entitled to.

It took me a long time to get this through my head because I came from a very authoritarian background. I thought that if anything was going to work, I would have to agree with it. I didn't have to be around very long before I discovered that these alcoholics were not only disagreeing with each other, they were seldom agreeing with themselves two days in a row. So, I took the next and much more inviting alternative. If I couldn't agree with everything I heard, then everybody else would have to agree with me.

Now this is an inviting alternative, and I pursued it for many years until it finally dawned on me that it doesn't work this way in Alcoholics Anonymous. I realized that, without any great design, we people who were forever living our lives on the basis of what somebody else thinks had come into a Fellowship where everybody tells us what they think ... but it's always different ... so somewhere along the line we are forced to think for ourselves, and that's the beginning of growing up.

In the next to the final paragraph in the book ALCOHOLICS ANONYMOUS there's a paragraph that I'd like to read to you because I want to set the tone for what we're going to be doing here.

What's the point of sobriety?

"Our book is meant to be suggestive only. We realize we know only a little. God will constantly disclose more to you and to us. Ask Him in your morning meditation what you can do each day for the man who is still sick. The answers will come, if your own house is in order. But obviously you cannot transmit something you haven't got. See to it that your relationship with Him is right and great events will come to pass for you and countless others. This is the Great Fact for us."[1]

What I would like to do for myself and with you is to see how you start to build a house that is in order where you can ask others to come in and have a little shelter from the wind and the cold. And I'm going to try to do it by reviewing four questions that came to me after I came to this Fellowship.

The first question is, as far as I'm concerned, the very heart and crux of what we are doing here and why we are not someplace else. It is the most promising question an alcoholic can ever ask himself because, depending upon the answer to it, it largely shapes the future of his life. And the question is *What the point of sobriety is?* Somewhere, sometime, if you haven't asked yourself that in those words, you will. Chances are you have done

---

[1] Page 164, ALCOHOLICS ANONYMOUS

The Rest of Your Life

it long before you got here. Of course, you probably haven't used the word *sobriety*. It seems to me that word never existed in my vocabulary until I had a 12th-step call made on me on February the 6th, 1952. When I first heard that word, I went into a state of shock. The minute I heard it, as drunk as I was, it brought a vision to me that has only slightly faded over the years, and that was a vision of a person who is in the pink of health but he is dead.

Now why would you and I look upon the mere fact of staying sober as something so wonderful that it should have some point to it? Well, I think it's because in our culture, sobriety is considered a virtue. Even on the part of non-alcoholics, abstaining from the fruit of the vine is often considered quite the thing to do. So if it is virtuous to do this, then it follows as the night to day that, (a) you have to be virtuous in order to do it and, (b) you should get, by God, a reward for it!

By the time the alcoholic reaches AA, this virtue has been held up to him as one of such shining dominance over all others that he wants something pretty big to happen if he goes along with this. It would be wonderful if we all discussed this expectation from the very beginning but apparently, somehow or other, we don't. That's why I'm trying to discuss it with you now because I think it's where it begins, it's where it stays, and finally, it's where it ends. When the alcoholic gets here, he can no longer look upon sobriety as a virtue no matter how difficult it might be

What's the point of sobriety?

or how many benefits he thinks are going to accrue from it. After he gets here, he finds out that what he has, this virtue that he thinks is something that is done by choice, and the lack of it on his part is a disease. When he isn't sober, he's sick! And he gets sicker and sicker the more he stays un-sober. He's been testing it for quite a while and he doesn't really believe the results most of the time.

I no longer had any quarrel with the results by the time I got here. I didn't go through any fingernail biting about whether I was an alcoholic at all. By the time I got here, I, and others, had called myself so many other names with such deadly accuracy, that the term alcoholic had a nice scientific sound. It sounded kind of upper class. In fact, it had a nice antiseptic ring to it. And when they assured me that I had a disease, I never really paid any attention because, the way I felt, whatever it is, whatever label you want to put on it, some terrible stigma or some nice euphemism, whatever, I've got it.

When we come to this Fellowship, most of us fall into two groups. The largest group says, "I will stay sober if I get back..." Now they have been around for a while and they have accrued and acquired things and they say this way down deep inside in the unconscious where it really counts. They never say this out loud because it would sound too crass. But they say it to themselves, "I will stay sober if I get back...," and there is a long list, depending upon the circumstances and background of the

The Rest of Your Life

individual. "I will stay sober if I get back my wife, if I get back my husband, if I get back my job, if I get back the car, if I get back the kids, if I get back my health, if I get back my self-respect, if I get back my figure…" and on and on.

I'm going to stop right now to define my terms because I want to forestall the tired old question of what is the difference between being dry and being sober. When I use the term *sobriety*, I am using it in the sense that it is the absence of any kind of chemical substance in your bloodstream that changes your thinking. Any substance, be it liquid or solid, and whether you take it through the mouth, in the veins, or some other way I haven't learned about. That's what I mean by *sobriety*. It just isn't there. You're not taking it anymore and you don't go off in a corner and ponder whether you are dry or sober. You just don't have any chemical inside of you that is changing your thinking.

Now, when you make this statement to yourself that "I will stay sober if I get back…and you have this long list that follows, very salutary things happen, great progress is often made. Generally old-timers look at these people and say, "My God, look how they're growing! " And they grow. Light comes into their eyes. They start making 12th step calls. Sobriety blossoms all over the place. And then without any warning, there comes a day, an hour, and they suddenly find themselves kind of ticking it off. "I stayed sober to get back…," and the things they stayed sober to get

What's the point of sobriety?

back either haven't gotten back or now that they have gotten back, they no longer want them. So, what course do you take at that point? You say to yourself, "What the hell is the point of sobriety?" That's what you say. And there's no point to sobriety if sobriety is going to be a means to an end and the end hasn't been gotten, or you no longer want it. So you dispense with it. Now that's one group.

The smaller group (maybe it's growing because they're coming in younger and younger and a lot haven't been around long enough to acquire very much to lose) says to themselves, "I will stay sober if I get a husband, if I get a wife, if I get a job, if I get a Cadillac, if I get the contract." And they grow. They stay sober. Great things happen. Months pass. Years can pass. Then one day its inventory time for them and what they have stayed sober to get either hasn't been gotten or now that they have gotten it, it has not the value that they thought so they in turn say, "What's the point of sobriety?" Since it didn't get them what they wanted, it has no point, no value in itself at all, so it is dispensed with. The virtue was followed. The virtue was practiced. We were virtuous while we were practicing it, but we didn't get our reward ... We didn't get our reward.

Now if you are an alcoholic, the "if I get..." is the most dangerous thinking that you can do. It so often happens to the newcomer this way because when he comes in, we define

The Rest of Your Life

alcoholism for him. We tell him that the physical part of this disease comes to a total, dead stop if he stays away from the first drink. Generally there will be a great nod of recognition to this statement. I remember the first time I heard it. I thought, "My God, why in the hell didn't I figure that out? Someone as brilliant as I am... that's the way you stay sober. You stay away from the first drink." And that's exactly the way you work the physical part. AA has no great formula or magic little kind of thing that you do in order to stay away from the first drink. You just stay away from it. Do anything else you want to. If you're a newcomer and you can still taste that drink in your mouth and I say to you, "There's only one way that you can stay sober and that is to stay away from the first drink," then that is *all* you have got to remember ... that is *all* you have got to remember.

I'm dwelling on this because sometimes at two or three o'clock in the morning I get a call. It's always nice to get a call at that hour and, generally, the voice on the other end is kind of towards the end of the second act. We haven't gotten into the third act yet where it's really going to get tragic, and it goes something like this. "Allen, I heard you talk and I sure as hell like what you say about letting the tailgater pass. Would you tell me more about that?"... And on and on. Finally I say, "How long have you been sober?" "Oh, I haven't been sober. I'm drinking, but I sure like what you say." Well, you see, anything I say is just *wind* unless

What's the point of sobriety?

you're going to stay away from the first drink. That's the name of this game. You don't come here to see me walk around making up a lot of nice things to say and then go out thinking, "By God, that's pretty good!" and then go down to the nearest bar or pick up a fifth on your way home. That isn't what this is all about. We are here for *one purpose* and *one purpose* only and that is: We are not going to drink anymore, we are not going to pop pills anymore, and we are not going to smoke pot anymore. This is the name of the game and how does it begin? It begins by staying away from the first drink or whatever you do with these different things you use. You are not going to do them anymore.

Now, you are going to say to me, "How do I do that?" You've done it before. We all have done it before. There's always been a day or an hour or an afternoon where we've stayed away from the first drink. Somebody or something kept us away from the first drink and that's all I'm saying to you. That's it. That's where it begins. I don't care about anything else you do. You don't have to be virtuous in order to do this. Generally we get you confused an awful lot of times. You come in here and we define alcoholism for you. We tell you you've got a disease. We tell you you've got to find a higher power. You've got to work 12 steps. You've got to go to meetings and you've got to do this and do that and pretty soon you think, "My God, get out the incense and the candles and let's go!" But you don't have to do any of this. ***You***

The Rest of Your Life

just have to stay away from the goddamn first drink! That is what you do. Now, do anything else like kick your wife, your husband, beat the kids, yell at the dog, and tell your boss you're resigning. Screw up your life however you want to, but don't take the first drink! Now, if that isn't clear, I don't know what else I can say.

So, if that's how you do it, then that's what makes it an end in itself. All comparisons are odious; all analogies never quite fit, but let me try to put it in another form. Let us suppose that, instead of alcoholism you have diabetes. You go to the doctor and you're examined and the tests are taken and then he comes in and says, "Well, I'm sorry to tell you, Joe, you have diabetes. And, as you know, you can die of diabetes. It can be a very, very serious disease, Joe. But you don't need to worry too much because there is a substance called insulin and if you take it regularly as I'm going to prescribe it to you, you will be able to live a normal life." And you go away with your insulin pills or syringe and after a while you come back to the doctor and say, "Doctor, I have decided not to take the insulin anymore. I've taken it exactly the way you prescribed, but my wife doesn't treat me any better than she used to. I still have the same trouble with my boss. My kids are driving me crazy. Taxes are too high. Nothing has changed, Doctor, nothing has changed, so why the hell should I take the insulin"? And then the doctor patiently says, "Joe, you take the insulin because that way you live"! And for the alcoholic,

What's the point of sobriety?

whether you like it or not, *you stay away from the first drink because that way you live.* Now, does that mean that if you continue to drink tonight, you will die tonight? No. It's too bad maybe that it isn't that way because my experience with progressive alcoholism is that it is fatal. But long before you die physically, everything that makes life worth living dies ... long, long before you die physically. And, in the almost 16 years that I've been in this Fellowship, I have had the unfortunate, sad experience of seeing many of the friends that were very close to me, come in here and leave, and they are still drinking, and they are dying by inches ... but they have lost everything that makes life worth living.

There is another thing I would like you to think about. Every human being, sometime in his life, somewhere in his life, is going to have to take a stand if he is ever going to grow up emotionally. If he's ever going to accept life on its terms, if he is ever going to face and recognize reality, then he is going to have to take a stand somewhere. He is going to have to put his feet down and do what in marketing we call "position the product." For an alcoholic there's a wonderful way if you've been on the run all your life and you have if you're an alcoholic. There is one way you can take a stand. It's so clear-cut. A lot of non-alcoholics, just as driven, just as neurotic, just as bugged, just as sure that there's no

The Rest of Your Life

way out, don't have as clear-cut a place where they can put their feet down and take a stand. But you do, just as I did one night.

I put my feet down and said, "Here I will stand. I will not take the first drink no matter what. I will not expect anything for it. I don't give a damn whether things are good or bad, whether I keep my job or lose my job, whether people hate me or love me, whether I finally flip my wig and really go insane and the boys in the little white jackets come and get me and take me away. At least, by God, I will know where I am going and who is taking me." And I put my feet down and I said it, not to God; there were no tears, there were no prayers, you don't need them, you don't need them to do this. You can do it yourself. You can put your feet down and say, "I may die here, I may collapse here, I may go crazy here, but from this spot I will not retreat." You can do it. I did it. Thousands of others have done it. And until you do it, you don't move forward. You keep moving backwards.

By now I hope that you have come to the conclusion that sobriety for an alcoholic is an end in itself. You have to quit thinking about it as a virtue. It has nothing to do with virtue. It has nothing to do with a reward. It has nothing to do with fringe benefits and dividends ... those phrases that we toss about like confetti in AA. The answer to the question, "What is the point of sobriety?" is "The point of sobriety is LIFE." It is as simple, it is as

What's the point of sobriety?

fundamental; it is as encompassing as that. The point of sobriety is life.

Remember that what I'm telling you are only my opinions, but I am telling them to you very vehemently because they are my vehement opinions. I don't have any mild opinions.

As your days in AA lengthen, you will hear a couple of phrases. One you don't hear much anymore, but I sure heard it because AA, as an organization, has only been in existence about 30 years and I've been around 16 of those, so I got in what we might call the early part. And when I got into AA, if you still had your own teeth, you were looked upon with a little suspicion. They thought maybe you hadn't suffered enough. Fingers were pointed at you and you were told; *staying sober is your number one problem.* Can you imagine how that sounds to the newcomer? When I heard that, I was dying to say to those old-timers (but I didn't want to displease them), "Why don't you come out with me to the parking lot of the 6300 Club and give me a couple of hours and I'll tell you what a few of my number one problems are?" But they were telling me the truth because I am an alcoholic, and while it is true that alcoholism is a symptom of deeper troubles, there is no point in getting into that until you have answered that first question, "What is the point of sobriety?"

The other phrase you hear, and it doesn't infuriate you quite as much ... sometimes it has kind of a wonderful, spiritual

The Rest of Your Life

and noble ring to it. It's said with a far-off look in the eyes, the head tilted up a little bit towards heaven. *For me sobriety alone is not enough.* Everybody kind of sighs and waits for all of the recitals, all the blessings that had to accompany this person's sobriety in order to make it worthwhile. Fine and dandy; I think that is great. As I have said, this is a Fellowship where everybody can believe what he wants to. But if sobriety alone is not enough, and all these blessings disappear, and they have a terrific way of coming and going, I tell you from 16 years of experience that sometimes they just aren't there at all and no AA program can guarantee you that they will be there. Sometimes they are so absent that you wonder why you ever started on this at all. So on those days when the sky is dark and you are looking in the mirror and you realize that you are not one whit different than you were several years ago, and these blessings that you thought you had were really wishful thinking, and these virtues that you thought you possessed were kind of being worn as a cloak in order to impress others and win for you the self-approval that you had been thirsting for all of your natural life, then what do you do? *Sobriety sure as hell better be enough at that moment or you will drink again.* And you will say the fatal words, "What the hell is the point of sobriety?"

That's the first question. I hope I've answered it and now I hope that I can answer some questions of yours.

What's the point of sobriety?

Question and Answer Period

When I was taking pills and booze I had power and I coped with reality. Now I am sober and I'm afraid to lick a postage stamp. Will there come a time, in sobriety, when I will have the same power to cope with reality that I had when I was full of booze and pills?

If you really had power in coping with reality, you wouldn't have needed pills or booze. There was a gnawing fear inside you that made you take pills and booze like it did with the rest of us. We didn't take them because we thought it was just a really rah-rah thing to do. If you're a very well, normal, well-adjusted person coping with reality and having a lot of power and getting along fine, you simply don't drink or pill yourself to death. You don't

The Rest of Your Life

have to come to AA. So the fear that you are now feeling sober, you are feeling because the things you were doing to hide it are absent. And the whole thing that AA tries to do, the whole goal of our therapy, is to change the thinking, change the emotion, and change the whole complex that has produced the fear that is now besetting you. So the answer is, if you are willing to put forth the effort required, if you are willing to do the things that have to be done, then the answer to your question is "yes." There does come a day, and sooner than you think, when sober, you are able to do what you had to get drunk to do before. And since you are doing them sober, you will do them a lot better. What's most wonderful about it is that you will remember doing them.

It's kind of difficult to mix with casual groups. I get queasy. When it's adults at meetings, it's okay, but with others or even AA's casual mixing, I feel ill at ease. Why?

The reason we all feel ill at ease sober at first is because we used to always feel ill at ease sober. So we got drunk in order that we wouldn't feel ill at ease sober. *That's why we drank.* We didn't know how to cope with what we thought was reality without some kind of aid. We did not know how to stand there, as ourselves,

What's the point of sobriety?

without a glass in our hand that would make us witty, charming, intelligent or brave, or sexy, or whatever we wanted to be on that particular night or day or afternoon. That's why we drank. Naturally when this artificial aid is removed, until we come to know ourselves, indeed can learn to have what the psychologists and the psychiatrists and the philosophers regard as the ultimate, plain *self-esteem* ... self-acceptance that leads to self-esteem ... then we're not comfortable no matter what group we're in.

I'll tell you how uncomfortable I was sober. And that's strange, too, because up until the last two years of my drinking, I was not a daily drinker. I was a periodic drinker. I didn't know I was a periodic. I never heard that phrase until I came to AA. I just drank when I couldn't stay sober and then I stayed sober as long as I could. And when I couldn't stay sober any longer, I drank again. The last few years of my drinking I drank pretty steadily. The periods became commas and the commas became comas. I used to stand outside an AA meeting or sit in the car and think, "Oh God, do I have to go in? And put on that face? And say hello?" I just used to hate it. I don't know why because I used to go to work a lot of times sober, but I never went to AA meetings sober. It took a long time for me to believe that AA was real. That's why I came in and I pretended ... I performed. I was one of the "I will stay sober if I get..." group. And God knows it wasn't because I was young and hadn't been around long enough to lose a few things. It was

The Rest of Your Life

simply because all I wanted was something very simple, very forthright, and very direct. I said to myself, way down deep here inside, "I will stay sober if I get *canonized*." That was all I wanted. But I wanted it while I was alive and could enjoy it. And I would have preferred it by acclamation. Well, it didn't come, and when it didn't, I said the fatal words, "What in the hell is the point of sobriety? What is the point of doing all this? Dragging myself to all these meetings, making these 12th-step calls on these dirty, smelly, lousy drunks. Listening to this crap that I had to listen to. Smiling at all these jerks. And I don't become a saint? What's the point of this? To hell with it." And I left. I resigned. Let me put it another way. Every art, every science, every philosophy has a basic premise upon which the whole structure rests. There's a Latin phrase that describes it. It is called the *sine qua non*. The literal translation of that is *without which, nothing else*. Now there is a sine qua non for recovery from alcoholism. It is the fact that sobriety is an end in itself. Whether it gets you anything, whether you feel comfortable or uncomfortable, sad or glad, afraid or brave, full of despair or full of hope, holy or bad, sinful or virtuous, chaste or unchaste, sobriety for the alcoholic is an end in itself. That is the fundamental requisite for recovery from this disease. Until you have that, you can stay sober for years and all you are doing in effect, in my opinion, is postponing a drunk. I have seen it happen again and again.

What's the point of sobriety?

What about resentments? I have 16 days.

Go ahead and have resentments. We give it to you so fast. Just stay away from the first drink. If you want to hate a few people, go ahead and hate them. See, you don't have to be virtuous in order to stay sober. As you go along, you will find that having resentments is uncomfortable, not to the person you resent, but to you. If you say, "I've got to get rid of the resentments or I'll get drunk," you will get drunk, because you will not get rid of the resentments. So, go ahead and have the resentments for a while. Stay away from the first drink.

I'm the reverse. I've 44 days and I love everything. How long is this beauty going to last?

See, with the alcoholic, you can't win. There's one who's worried because he hates everybody and there's one who's worried because he loves everybody. The answer for you is exactly the answer I gave him. If you're feeling good, enjoy it ... enjoy it ... don't question it, it will go away in time.

I feel like a beginner. I had two life-long ambitions. One was material, a motorcycle. The other was to play in a high-class jazz joint and there are only two of those in town. Tuesday night I

The Rest of Your Life

played in one and I got the motorcycle I've wanted all my life. And it doesn't get it. Neither one gets it and I feel that this is growth, that nothing outside is going to get it anymore. When do I get it inside?

You always have to open the door before you go through it. And when you have opened the door, as you just have, of discovering that material things or status, playing in a jazz joint or owning a motorcycle do not of themselves bring you happiness, then you have opened the door to getting it inside. Now, you will go through that door. But you have already started. I have found in my life that questions that are uppermost in my mind at any given time, those that are bugging me, are always in the process of being answered in my daily life or they would not be bugging me. Pretty soon I find that I have worked through to the answer. It is one of the most encouraging things I have ever found. Things that keep coming back in my mind, bugging the daylights out of me, after a while I find that I have been living the answer. The answer has been coming out of this turmoil and that's why the questions have been bugging me. This is what's happened to you.

Again, let's get back to the newcomer. You come in here and one thing you're sure of is that life is pretty grim. We start talking to you and telling you that life can be beautiful. You don't believe it and you think this is an act like I did when I first

What's the point of sobriety?

came. My first reaction to AA was that it wasn't real. I didn't know that at the time. I just felt uncomfortable, and one of the big reasons I felt uncomfortable was that I didn't believe in any of it. I didn't believe that the people were real and certainly I didn't believe what I was hearing was real. I read the book and I didn't have any quarrel with it and I thought it was completely sound. I think the confusion persists because we begin to talk to you so often about things that can only begin to make sense to you after you have had a certain period of sobriety. Now I know this is all insult to your intelligence. But what we're talking about to you is that you try, just try to start beginning to be willing to look at something you have never looked at before in your life and that is yourself. You have thought that you have looked at yourself because you have been completely preoccupied with yourself. You have been sick with self-centeredness. But you've only been concerned about yourself; you have not looked at yourself. You have not come to grips with yourself and that takes a little time.

Stay away from the first drink. The point of sobriety is life itself and that condition is fulfilled for itself alone, not in order to see if other things will come. You fulfill it only if you wish to keep alive. If you don't want to live, then drink. Death will be a long time coming and it will be very messy. But if you wish to live, and you are an alcoholic, then you have passed the point when you can any longer choose about this. You call only choose either

The Rest of Your Life

to be drunk or to be sober. You can't choose any happy medium. The "happy medium day" has gone. You have to choose to be either drunk or sober, and you will decide in favor of sobriety only if and when you value being sober more than you value being drunk. For our purposes we've now got to assume that you have made that decision for sobriety. If you haven't, then the rest of the things that we talk about are just exercises in air. Go to the ball game and sit outside. It's healthy. There is no point sitting around here brooding and turning this rigorous honesty in on yourself and coming up with all kinds of horrible answers. You don't stay sober by sitting around contemplating the sunset or doing any of the things I used to do and stay drunk. You just stay away from the first drink and you do not have to be walking with your hand in God's in order to do this. What you have to do is just don't open the bottle and don't take the drink.

It was so strongly in my mind that sobriety was a virtue that I had it down to a very clear alternative. If you were not in a state of grace, then the only other state to be in was a state of drunkenness. There was no middle ground. Now I have Irish-Catholic friends all over the country who are still doing this. They get in touch with me regularly. They still don't understand why I'm staying sober because they contend that I am no better than they are and they are right. I just value sobriety and I have not got it mixed up any longer with the state of grace.

Is a Spiritual Experience Necessary?

SESSION 2
July 11, 1968

The Rest of Your Life

Is a Spiritual Experience Necessary?

Is a Spiritual Experience Necessary?

LET'S NOW try to use a very overworked but apt cliché that points out what sobriety has become to the alcoholic. Sobriety is like soil to the farmer who has to bring in a crop or go broke. If he has a farm and good soil, he has to cultivate it, let it lie fallow and feed it. There has to be some rain, and finally, there is a harvest. But without the soil, the ground, the earth, nothing would happen. And yet the earth, of itself, cannot bring forth a harvest. Sobriety is the foundation of the rest of your life, but it cannot of itself bring you very much more than good health and a better brain to think with, not that they should be minimized for they can take you far. So, if sobriety is our foundation, then let's take another question.

What are we doing here in AA if really all you have to do is stay sober and to stay sober is to stay away from the first drink, This is a legitimate question and I've asked it of myself

The Rest of Your Life

many times. I hope that I'm shocking you with this because until you get this in your head, You can get all confused with whether or not you're having a spiritual experience or a spiritual awakening, whether or not you're doing it right, whether you're working the program, whether you're on the program or off the program and the next thing you know, it's all added up to, there's nothing else to do but get drunk. And there is no reason in the world to get drunk. Nobody's so bad that he can't stay away from the first drink and no alcoholic's so good that he can afford not to. It's as simple as that.

Is *a spiritual experience necessary to sobriety?* I've answered it factually, *no.* Remember, I'm speaking only for myself, but I hope that you think about this a lot because, if you can buy it, then your sobriety is as secure as the air you breathe. Your sobriety is independent of anything else except your staying away from the first drink and if you're sober now, you are doing it so you know it can be done.

Then why would we come to meetings like this', Why would we have this book? Why would we have twelve steps? What would be the point to this whole business? Finally there comes a question that we have got to ask ourselves, *Why did I drink*? What made it necessary for me to become an alcoholic? Why was it when I found out that this liquid or these pills or whatever

Is a Spiritual Experience Necessary?

chemical substance that I was using was doing a lot more than I bargained for, why didn't I leave it alone?

The answers are as numerous as the people who drank. A lot of them come down to five, six, seven answers, but when you put them all into a Bunsen burner and distill it, it comes down to the essence. *The reason you drank and the reason I drank to alcoholic excess was that we wanted to change our reaction to what we thought was reality.* I would say that we wanted to change our reaction to reality, but you will find out, as I found out, that we didn't even know what reality was. There was always some kind of change involved. We wanted to get from where we were emotionally or mentally to someplace else and it didn't work. We were never content to sit where we were in reality. It was move over here or move over there. A change had to be involved. If we were being peaceful, we wanted to be uproarious. If we were being uproarious, we wanted to be paralyzed. If we were in good health, we wanted to be sick. If we were sick, we wanted to be healthy. We always took this booze in order to change our reaction because we found out that the reality didn't change. Our attitude towards it changed.

So what are we going to do here in AA? We are going to come up with a non-chemical technique that will change our attitude toward what we think is reality.

The Rest of Your Life

Now, along those lines, let's define our terms. What is a spiritual experience? When I came into AA the Appendix to the book ALCOHOLICS ANONYMOUS had not been written and the terms, *spiritual experience*, and *spiritual awakening*, were said with a great deal of awe. There were always invisible quotes around them and they quivered like papers and you said them softly, trying not to look at anybody. You always said them with your eyes turned up because, naturally, you wanted everybody to feel that you were there ... or on the verge of one ... or having another one. A lot of people had them on the hour by the hour. I remember when they used to be called, at the 6300 Club, manifestations, and by God, they came in there at all hours of the day and night with them. So the newcomer got the idea that nothing was going to work without them. Nobody said, "Just stay away from the first drink and if you never have a spiritual experience for the rest of your life and go on hating yourself and the whole world around you, you can still do it sober." A lot of times you can hate a lot better sober and think up things to do to drive people crazy. You don't get caught so often either. But the newcomer would get the feeling that he was going to have to wake up on a mountaintop feeling a clean wind sweeping though film. He was going to have to one-day stand there and there would be "that light" and then everything would be all right. It was kind of sad because in those days a lot of people who had the clean wind

Is a Spiritual Experience Necessary?

sweeping through them found it was sweeping them out too. They didn't hang around very long.

Finally we got out an Appendix and I want to read it to you because it will define our terms.

"The terms 'spiritual experience' and 'spiritual awakening' are used many times in this book which, upon careful reading, shows that the personality change sufficient to bring about recovery from alcoholism has manifested itself among us in many different forms.

"Yet it is true that our first printing gave many readers the impression that these personality changes, or religious experiences must be of the nature of sudden and spectacular upheavals. Happily for everyone, this conclusion is erroneous.

"In the first few chapters a number of sudden revolutionary changes are described. Though it was not our intention to create such an impression, many alcoholics have nevertheless concluded that in order to recover they must acquire an immediate and overwhelming God-consciousness followed at once by a vast change in feeling and outlook.

The Rest of Your Life

"Among our rapidly growing membership of thousands of alcoholics such transformations, though frequent, are by no means the rule. Most of our experiences are what the psychologist William James calls the 'educational variety' because they develop slowly over a period of time. Quite often friends of the newcomer are aware of the difference long before he is himself. He finally realizes that he has undergone a profound alteration in his reaction to life..."[2]

Now from here on, let's use that as our definition of the terms *spiritual experience* and *spiritual awakening*. It is a change in your response, in your attitude to life ... a change, a non-chemical change in how you respond to the world around you, the people in it, and to yourself.

If we take that as a definition, the next question is "How do we go about it," This is where the therapy of AA comes in. Where do you make a beginning in changing, permanently, how you have been reacting to life? The AA prayer says, "God grant me the serenity to accept the things I cannot change," so already we know there must be some things we can't change, "Courage to

---

[2]Page 569, ALCOHOLICS ANONYMOUS

Is a Spiritual Experience Necessary?

change the things we can, and the wisdom to know the difference." This wisdom comes very quickly because, after looking back upon a lifetime of trying to change others, I think that one of the first things that can be gotten across to you is that changing others is pretty impossible and that the persons who are going to have to be changed are you and I.

The principles set forth in AA are not new. They are as old as our civilization and certainly there are in them the basic principles of every kind of spiritual approach to life. What is the new thing that AA found and added? Probably without knowing it, they had found the keystone. That keystone pertains to the things that we are going to try to learn to do here, tied up in the phrase that you will hear over and over again in meetings because it's contained in the preamble to Chapter Five. It says "rigorous self-honesty." It wasn't too impossible for us as practicing alcoholics to stand back and size up the situation as it applied to other people and other facts. If it had been totally impossible for us to do this, we probably wouldn't have earned a living, we wouldn't have been successful at all; we wouldn't have managed at all. Somewhere back at an early age, we would have probably been institutionalized because we would have been out of touch with reality. We would not have been able to deal with it. So, however ineffectively we were dealing with it, at least it kept us going.

The Rest of Your Life

Wherein then did our handicap lie? Was it when we turned this evaluation in upon ourselves, when we tried to assess our role, when we tried to look at ourselves and fit ourselves into the picture? But this is the whole trick of what we call growing up. Emotional maturity is the acceptance of self which finally leads to the correct evaluation of self which would finally lead, we hope, to self-esteem. So really, the new thing that's been added to AA is the phrase "self-honesty." It was that a therapy arose whereby people would apply this honesty, one to the other, because that's how it began. It didn't begin in a book. It didn't begin in a great big, huge meeting like this. It didn't begin with somebody like me standing up with a neck microphone and making with the words. It began with two frightened, terribly ashamed, terribly guilty, terribly confused, and terribly despairing human beings who got together and because they were so frightened, so full of fear, and so at the breaking point, that they began to tell the truth to each other. They told the truth to each other.

This telling of the truth from one human being to another, on a man to man basis, without benefit of sacraments or priests or ministers, without any ritual or any kind of dogma or documents, just two human beings stripping themselves naked in front of each other and, by trusting each other, becoming willing to be totally vulnerable, willing to stand there before another human being, often a total stranger and saying, "This is me. This is

Is a Spiritual Experience Necessary?

everything I wish to God that I wasn't. This is me and I am telling it to you and I trust you and I hope that you won't hurt me." This is how it began and this is the way I think it will have to continue because this is the way we get ready for it. To me the very epitome of the 12 principles of AA is contained in the fourth and fifth steps. Everything prior to that is preparation for those steps and everything after is the implementation of what we found and what we decide.

Let's go back now and take the first, second and third steps if they are a preparation. Nobody can work any of the AA steps for you, it's a personal experience. It goes as deep as you are willing to go. In AA, as in every other therapy, the patient is always the doctor. The patient sets the pace. The patient says how far he will go, how much therapy will be applied and how well he will get. Nobody can push him because he has to do it himself. So, if he is going to say, *I admitted that I was powerless over alcohol and that my life was unmanageable*, this has to be something that he believes.

Now I found that admitting that my life was unmanageable seemed a little inaccurate. Then I found that if I substituted a word that was much more accurate for me, because it was what I was trying to keep hidden, it was easier for me. It was more accurate as far as I was concerned. I said to myself, "I admit that I am powerless over alcohol and that my emotions are

The Rest of Your Life

unmanageable." This is what I could never really predict. I could predict that I would be at work, but I could never predict how I was going to feel. I could never predict how I was going to perform. I never could predict whether or not I would stay. So it was my emotions; how I reacted to what was going on around me that finally became completely and totally unmanageable. So unmanageable that it seemed to me that the only alternative was to try to withdraw from life and the only acceptable way for me, with my religious background and belief, was to die a drunk. There's always a chance that you will be diagnosed as something else. That was why I always used to like to specify a sanatorium close to St. Ambrose Church on Fairfax, because I figured that if I was in the sanatorium that was only two blocks away, it might all work out one day that the doctor would arrive with a shot of paraldehyde and Father O'Toole would come with the last sacraments at the same time and I would be what was called *saved!*

Came to believe that a Power greater than ourselves could restore us to sanity. Nobody can take this step for you. In AA we don't attempt to define this Power. I came in with a very, very arranged God. He had been around for centuries and He had been painted and drawn, interpreted and dogmatized, and He was down in books and every place else and I was sure His servant and I was scared to death. I said I loved Him and everything was going fine and I realize now, after 16 years of sobriety and quite a little

Is a Spiritual Experience Necessary?

bit of therapy and work along with the years of sobriety, that I don't know anything at all about this Power greater than myself. I don't know whether I understand Him or not. I have a feeling that if I understood Him, He wouldn't be God. He and I would just kind of be buddies. He would be just Mr. Glad, I guess ... or Mr. Clean, whichever I happened to need at the time. But I don't know anything about Him at all, so I can't help you.

I used to be able to give you quite a dissertation, just mention God and if you showed any kind of doubt, I could take you off and straighten you out. But now I'm not so sure I understand Him. I don't ever expect to, but I am content to choose to believe that if He is around, He understands me. And that should keep Him occupied as far as I'm concerned. I'm willing to take my chances with Him. I have evidence in my life that He can restore you to sanity, however He goes about it or whether He's involved or not. If you go along and keep taking one more step and you don't throw in the towel, no matter how much you want to, sooner or later more sanity than I ever had before came, and that's quite a bit.

Made a decision to turn our will and our lives over to the care of God as we understood Him. That's the thing again that I had been doing with deadening regularity all of my life. I did it every morning except mornings, naturally, when I was in a state of sin, and there's no use turning your life over to God when you're

The Rest of Your Life

in a state of sin. You keep it to yourself those mornings. You sure as hell ain't going to let God move in on those times because it's only when you finally say goodbye to that life that you move over. And so it was this Dr. Jekyll and Mr. Hyde life I had going that was just like changing underwear except that towards the end, I got mixed tip, I never knew what suit I was wearing.

But what do we mean when we say, "Turn our life and our will over to Him?" I'll tell you what it doesn't mean to me. It doesn't mean, as I used to think, that I had to sit, from that moment forward, and wait until little celestial beep-beeps came through and said, "go left," "go right," "get up," "sit down," "go to work," "come home." I finally learned it meant that I was to use whatever gifts I had been given. I was going to have to work with the clay I had. All my life I was really like a sculptor who knew he could sculpt but he always felt that he couldn't find the right clay.

If he could just find a better grade of clay, then he could sculpt something worthy of his efforts and worthy of his talents and worthy of him. So he spent a lifetime looking for the clay and finally one day he died and there wasn't even an epitaph for him. Maybe the epitaph was, "He didn't find the right clay." I finally decided that, if I'm going to turn my will and my life over to the care of God and I am where I am on that particular day, in that particular situation, and in that particular state of mind, that must be where I was going to have to begin. I am going to have to

Is a Spiritual Experience Necessary?

begin *where He has me now*. And that's where any human being has to begin ... wherever he is. You can't go back and start out where you wish you could. The journey has to begin from where you are now. And it has to keep beginning there. Every time there is a snag, or the ship founders a little bit or gets blown off course, you have to begin again from where you are.

This leads us to the fourth and fifth steps. There are all kinds of rules and guides and it's very carefully treated in the *12 and 12*... suggestions and recommendations on how to take your first inventory. There are two things I want to add. First, don't overlook writing it. It says to write it and I didn't write it because I had been in the habit of not writing it. I had been taking inventories all my life and my books were always so current that it never really bothered me ... I just carried them around on my back. The files were always in my head, always being gone through. But there is a terrific trauma that you need to put down in black and white. Try to spare yourself the euphemisms that you will want to come up with. The beautiful sweet terms that you will want to use instead of saying that you kicked the hell out of your wife. A little marital difficulty is a nice euphemism. Don't do it that way. Put it down in black and white so you can look at it in words of one syllable.

And if you say, "I don't know how to begin," begin with when you started feeling guilty and that will be a long, long time ago. So give yourself a lot of paper and a lot of time and go

The Rest of Your Life

someplace and do this. I would suggest that, if you're a newcomer, don't try it for at least thirty days. Not that you need to take this advice. Some of you couldn't be hogtied and kept from taking your inventory. You're looking forward to it with glee. Others will say five years later, "I don't know, I don't seem to be able to do it." Which proves that all you need to do to stay sober is to stay away from the first drink. I like to keep repeating that!

The reason I say to stay sober at least thirty days before you take pen in hand is because, for thirty days, you're not sure whether you're guilty or if you've been put upon. You're not sure about anything. You're not sure if you want to stay, sit, run or fly. If you want to put it off for a little while longer, so be it, but don't put it off too long. Not that you're going to get drunk because the only thing that will get you drunk is to take the first drink. So don't say that "I got drunk because I didn't take my inventory or I didn't write it or I didn't use the right color ink. You get drunk because you take a drink and decide to take a drink. No one comes and hands it to you. There's nobody with a little doll image of you, sticking pins in it. We've tried that in AA and it doesn't work. Nobody has been able to get anybody else drunk, no matter how many little voodoo images we've made. Nobody got drunk except the people who wanted to get drunk. So, don't put your inventory off too long, but don't do it too soon.

Is a Spiritual Experience Necessary?

Then you say, "What am I going to put down?" If you started back as far as when you began to feel guilty, then doesn't it follow that you put down what makes you feel guilty, what makes you feel ashamed, what makes you feel so terribly disappointed in yourself, what makes you feel so very frightened? And, if you can, end up with those things that you would rather die than have any other human being know. Now they al- ways turn out to be not nearly the terrible, horrible, reprehensible things that immediately come into people's minds. They always turn out to be some things that have bugged you all your life. Some time when you were probably terribly, terribly cowardly or weak or ashamed. Put them down.

After you're finished, then it would be a good time to sit and think about it a little while longer instead of rushing out to find somebody to share it with. Consider the person carefully. The only thing it stipulates is another human being and the only thing I would add is that if possible, whether it be a priest, a doctor, a lawyer, a psychologist, a friend, another AA member, try to choose somebody whom you feel will be able to help you look at this neither condoning nor condemning, because you will tend to go one way or the other in this fifth step and you've got to cut a middle road.

We started out tonight with the question: *Is a spiritual experience necessary for sobriety?* I believe, and it is my opinion

The Rest of Your Life

that I will take to the grave based on my experience and the experience of countless others, that the answer to that question is no. So don't try to build yourself an alibi. Staying away from the first drink has nothing to do with whether you are having a spiritual experience or anything else. It has to do with whether or not you, as an alcoholic, value being sober more than you value being drunk. It's as simple as that. Now then, if that's the answer to the question, can we go on and extend the question a little bit further? If sobriety is our foundation, the indispensable foundation to the house that we're going to try to build and will spend the rest of our lives building, is a spiritual experience necessary to raise this superstructure above ground zero? I believe that the answer to that question is *yes*

Is a Spiritual Experience Necessary?

Question and Answer Period

Once you have taken the fourth and fifth steps in the manner prescribed and recommended in the book and in the principles and therapy of AA, is it necessary to do it again?

I think that this is a very important question. If you take an inventory in this way, as prescribed and recommended; you take it from a moral viewpoint. You are reviewing your life for a very good reason and a very good purpose, and you are reviewing it from the standpoint of a moral right or a moral wrong. I don't think you will ever have to do this again because there will no longer be any need to keep going back and weighing the guilt and the shame. I spent a lifetime picking at the sores of my past and I don't think there's anything more destructive or corrosive than this. It doesn't get rid of the guilt. It doesn't exorcise the guilt at all. It just

The Rest of Your Life

deepens it. After you have done this as thoroughly as you can, at whatever stage of sobriety you are in, and you have written this and have taken this fifth step with another human being, then forget about it. The only other time that you will refer back to your past is to learn from it and you will try to do that, hopefully, from a non-moral viewpoint. All question of right or wrong will now be left out because You have fulfilled the conditions. Now You can go back and review your life to learn the pattern of behavior...what you were after...why you were doing what you were doing, and what you were hoping to gain.

Don't you think that the tenth steps more of a continuation of the fourth and fifth steps?

Yes of course, but it's supposed to be on a daily basis and therefore it shouldn't be as traumatic an experience as the fourth and fifth steps. The tenth step really is a daily extension of the basic thing that we're talking about, of the new thing that was added of rigorous self-honesty. It just keeps going along those lines. The tenth step is supposed to be a daily step.

"We continued to take a personal inventory and when we were wrong promptly admitted it." This is where I think a great deal of the troubles come from ... when we keep going back. Again and again I hear, "Allen, what do you do about the guilt? What do

Is a Spiritual Experience Necessary?

you do about the shame"? Well, you have done it. If you do the fourth and fifth steps, then the moral part of that guilt, any of the right or wrongness of it, you have done all that you can do. And you leave it alone. From now on, you are going to look for what was behind those things. They were not just acts that you chose out of the clear blue sky to fling in the face of God and man. You chose them very, very deliberately.

How do we practice rigorous self-honesty?

We assume that if we use the phrase, we've got it. If it were that easy we would have been practicing it all of our lives. This is why the fourth and fifth steps are the beginning. I knew my acts. There they were in front of me. If I lost my temper, if I cut somebody down to size, if I lashed out at somebody, if I got drunk, if I slept around ... all of these things ... there they were. And I said, "I did that." Now, that's honest. The self-honesty comes in when you try to understand why. When you look inside yourself and say, "Why did you do this"? Then when the answers come, this is the self that you have been trying to keep hidden, that you've been putting away, that you have not wanted anybody else to find out and therefore, you've kept it hidden from yourself. The self that you have repressed all these years. The self that reacted to reality and caused you to want to drink. This is the self-honesty that you have

The Rest of Your Life

to turn your eyes into, and comes, I think, only from a searching analysis practiced over and over again of ... Why?

Isn't this one of the most important reasons for sponsorship? At 16 years I'm sure or reasonably sure, that you probably see things about Allen that were not honest a year ago that you thought were honest at the time. Don't you need someone outside yourself in order to find rigorous self-honesty?

I don't want to put it down to sponsorship. I think you need help. That's why we're here, so this help has to come from somebody else. Help is all around us. We're in AA because we want and expect help from our fellow members. Naturally, this is one of the roles a sponsor should fill. But I don't believe that a sponsor should immediately start doing all your thinking for you. Everybody is a source of help and I don't think you should shut out any avenue or therapy or technique that will make you more able to do this.

Did you, in taking your inventory, search for the good in you?

Yes, but I didn't spend much time on it because I had already concluded that it was a futile search and this was very, very wrong. Back again to the self-honesty; just as you were concerned with the

Is a Spiritual Experience Necessary?

guilt and the bad, the wrong and the undesirable, I think you have to be equally concerned with why there is good. Why do you have the assets that you have as well as the liabilities?

How do you get rid of resentful attitudes even though they may be very minor?

Minor resentments always build into major resentments. They are self-perpetuating. There is only one way in the world that I have been able to get rid of resentments. I have tried praying them away and smiling them away. I have tried pretending them away and kissing them away. Nothing worked for me except trying to figure out in what way the person I resent poses a threat to me. How does this person threaten me? Does this person have something that I want for myself? Does he or she in some way diminish me? Am I envious? Am I jealous? Sometimes we use this word resentment and we're not being accurate. I don't think you can have a resentment against any human being, (I'm not talking about disliking someone ... there are bound to be people who bug you. We're talking about those who really get under your skin and cause you to be uncomfortable) unless, in some way, they pose a threat to you. You are envious of them, you are jealous of them, or

The Rest of Your Life

you are afraid of them. There's some way they have power over you and they pose a threat to you. I've said many times that one of the funniest ways to watch the truth of this is if a third party can tell the resenter, "Well gee, that's odd, he speaks very well of you!" And your resentment will vanish.

You get drunk after years. You've failed and you're trying again. Do you take this inventory again?

Yes. Something was wrong the first time so it won't hurt to review. If you were around thirty years and went out and you're back, I'd take the inventory again. There's no harm in starting from scratch.

How do you know when you're ready to take your inventory?

You're ready when you would like to start changing the kind of person you are. Until that time, there's not much point in taking an inventory, is there?

What Are the Old Ideas?

Session 3
July 18, 1968

The Rest of Your Life

What Are the Old Ideas?

What Are the Old Ideas?

THE LAST TWO weeks we have been asking ourselves how we build a house of sobriety. Our book tells us to see to it that our house is in order and great events will come to pass for us and countless others. I put before us questions that have certainly figured largely in my sobriety, questions that have come up again and again in my relations with my companions on this road of happy destiny over the years.

The first question was, "What is the point of sobriety?" You ask it many, many times before you get here and, believe me; you ask it many, many times after you get here. Certainly this is the question that the newcomer often contemplates and until he's

The Rest of Your Life

answered this question, everything else that I, or any other member of AA say from the podium or even privately is largely wind in the trees. We can discuss old ideas, spiritual experiences, the steps, and the book; but until you are staying away from the first drink, it's largely exercise. The answer to that question is that, if you are an alcoholic, the point of sobriety is simply that you have chosen to live.

Last week we took the question a step further and asked, "Is it necessary to have a spiritual experience in order to maintain sobriety?" And we found that the answer to that, technically and theoretically, is "no." You don't have to be virtuous, you don't have to be spiritual, and you don't have to be anything to accomplish the physical act of staying away from the first drink. If you can keep that in your mind, you have removed an alibi for your future drinking that is a great alibi. How many people have rationalized that first drink by saying, "Well, I can't do it; I can't work the steps; I can't get the peace and serenity and spiritual well-being that everybody else has, so I get drunk." This is what it is, a rationalization. Today I talked to two people on the telephone. They ranged in sobriety from four months to five years and both of them were about as dejected and despondent as two people could get. And yet each of them knew, as we talked, that it was in their power to stay away from the first drink ... that they could do it. Whether they want to do it or not is in their hands.

What Are the Old Ideas?

However, if we take the definition of spiritual experience that is given in the appendix of the book ALCOHOLICS ANONYMOUS, which is that this is not a great awakening ... not a great religious experience ... not a sweeping of the winds from the mountaintop through every pore of your body, then the answer to that question is "yes." It is a gradual change in your reaction to life ... to reality ... in the way that you react to the world around you ... to yourself and to life as it comes to you. The answer is "yes," if there's going to be any change. If you were drunk and miserable and now are going to be sober and miserable, then you don't need a spiritual experience. But if you want to make some kind of a change and have this life that you have chosen to live be more for the living, then there absolutely has to be a spiritual experience. Remember that I'm using the definition in no religious sense whatever. It is a change that comes about through what you do, through the steps you take, the thinking and meditating you do, and the effort you put forth.

We then considered how the AA program begins this and we took the steps, one through five. One more thing I wish I had it engraved on my head and then I wouldn't have to say it all the time ... or maybe had a little sign that sticks up behind me. I do not speak officially for Alcoholics Anonymous and neither does anyone else, including the founders. There is no official viewpoint. Even the book is suggestive, as it points out over and over again.

The Rest of Your Life

So, if anything I say distresses you, the simplest thing to do is ignore it. There is no point in being distressed because there is no orthodoxy in AA. All I'm doing is what everybody else does ... put suggestions before you based on my own experience and the experience of others. So please keep that in mind. Anything I say can be held against me, but it can't be held against AA.

Now let's suppose that we have taken steps one through five. We didn't take them to the best of our ability because we'll later find that there ain't no such thing, but we took them. That's the important thing. We took them and we left the perfection of our taking them in the hands of a Power greater than ourselves. What generally happens to most of us when we finish and wipe the perspiration of humility from our brow ... well, we make Tiny Tim look like a sorehead. For the ones who have never done it before, the reaction is absolutely miraculous. I think that this is where die phrase that you hear so much when you come into AA comes from ... what you call "the honeymoon" or "cloud nine." I always thought that when they talked about the honeymoon in AA you had found yourself a sober partner. Of course, if you have done this before, then the reaction is less. I didn't get such a terrific ecstatic bang out of it because, from my background, I had been doing a reasonable facsimile of this for a long, long time with, I might add, no noticeable peace of mind ensuing. But for most people it's a really wonderful thing. The lull

What Are the Old Ideas?

goes off, a deep breath is taken, life is changed, you feel cleansed, and suddenly everything is good ... the wife, the kids, the job ... you wonder what the hell you were so bugged about before? Everything is great. Everything is fine.

Then, little by little by little, the light in the eyes dims. The snarl begins to replace the smile. A little thing called hostility begins to rear its ugly head and then comes the question, "What the hell is the matter? I did everything. I wrote it all down. I went and found this jerk and I told everything to him or her and I've been making amends and I've been doing all these other things and I feel like hell. What's more, I'm not really any better." Now, how could that be? I think there are three reasons and I'll put them out for you. As I said, before I got here I had been doing this for a long, long time in the religion that I was born and brought up in except you didn't write it down. You were supposed to know it well enough not to have to write it down. You didn't need to write it down because you did it so often.

I think one of the commonest reasons for this happening is that you are coming face to face now, day after day after day, with a little thing called reality. It may not be reality as you will later find it to be, as you will later come to know it, but nevertheless, you are not hauling off and taking leave via booze or pills. You are not dismissing the whole thing in a vapor of booze or some other kind of chemical substance that's going to change your

The Rest of Your Life

thinking. You stand there. You've taken a stand and you have quit running physically, let us say, and you have set things there. Life is there day after day and you find that after all you have done, life remains pretty much the same.

One of the great discoveries that you will make here, sooner or later, is that AA offers you no immunity from the slings and arrows of outrageous fortune. They will occur. Life has a way of seeing that they do, and just because you're in here and we've got some steps and we're all staying sober together doesn't mean that we now have an invisible armor that we go through life with and never again have a worry. The trouble is that this is what most of us have been looking for all of our lives. I certainly was looking for it. I wanted to find that day, that thing, that sacrament, or that combination of prayers that would put this thing on me and by God, the arrows would just fall off. That's all there was going to be ... I'd win through.

Another reason might be that we are discovering the great fallacy that, a virtue assumed is not a virtue acquired. Now this comes as a great shock because you have been taught that this is so. How many times have you been taught, "Practice humility if you want to be humble?" The other day I was talking to a guy who had been sober about four months and he said, "You know, Allen, how I'm handling everything up to now? At the slightest sign of anything going wrong, I say, 'I'm sorry, forgive me.'" Then he

What Are the Old Ideas?

drew a deep breath and said, "But I don't know how long I can keep it up." And I wanted to laugh and I wanted to cry because it was like a tape recorder of my past.

I remember the first three months that I was here, preparing myself for canonization. One day I was walking down the corridor of my office and the way it was arranged, the acoustics were such that, even when people were talking in normal voices, it was as though a sound system carried down the corridor. As I was walking toward a particular office, I heard this guy say, "Here comes McGinnis and he's got that look again; he's going to apologize." That was true. I spent months just apologizing. It didn't occur to me whether or not anybody wanted this or expected this. I just went around apologizing. I thought, "This is very good. This is money on the bank. Now, in case I finally haul off and hit somebody, I will have apologized to them first" We have been doing this all of our lives. We're taught to do it and we're taught that it works. We ignore all the evidence to the contrary because that would shake the foundations of our belief and we'll get to that a little bit later.

What could be the third reason? Could it be that we find that this guilt that we thought we had gotten rid of by taking all these steps…by turning our life and our will over to the care of a Power greater than ourselves, by taking a written inventory and admitting to God, to ourselves, and to another human being… is not gone? Logically, that should get rid of the guilt, but unfortunately, we're not. We're not dealing with logical guilt, we're dealing with emotions.

What we have after we put aside the physical allergy that alcoholism develops is an emotional disease. We are emotionally troubled, emotionally ill. Let's define that so we'll all know that we're talking about the same thing. What is an emotion? *An emotion is a physical response to a thought.* You have to have a thought first before you can have an emotion. The emotion is a reaction to it. So we have been emotionally ill in our thinking. The guilt that we have been feeling has had nothing to do with logic, although we have put a lot of logical guilt with it. Way, way back before the logical guilt came along, there was a subjective guilt. How did that come about?

A sentence in the book says, *"Many of us tried to hang onto our old ideas and the result was nil until we let go absolutely."*[3] Let's talk then about old ideas. The old ideas that are behind these emotions, that are behind these acts that are behind these feelings that haunt us, that torment us, that bug us, that come back again and again and again. After we've taken the fourth step, after we've taken the fifth step, and after we've taken the tenth step, again and again they come back. Why? Could it be that they began long before there was any logic? Every human being who

---

[3] Page 58, ALCOHOLICS ANONYMOUS

What Are the Old Ideas?

walks through the door of this AA meeting or any other AA meeting and, as a matter of fact, probably every human being who walks through the door of a cathedral, the door of a church, a synagogue or temple, or the door of a psychiatrist's office for the first time, all have one great thing in common. Deep down inside of us we are consumed with self-hatred, self-condemnation, and self-abnegation. No matter what our outward appearance is and no matter what the facts of our life are ... no matter how successful we've been or how much money we have in the bank ... how many kids we have, or dollars or cars or whatever, or how many people look at us and say, "My God, what could that guy hate himself about?" deep down inside there is this total conviction that we are unworthy. We don't deserve anything. What we deserve is doom and perdition. Where did it come from? Does it have anything to do with logic? I think not. I'm talking about what I've come to believe about me and putting it out to see if it finds an echo in you. God knows I have found all echo in a lot of people whom I've talked to over the years.

Everybody I've talked to in AA, every alcoholic, (when we got down to sharing) had childhoods nearly always the same. No matter what the circumstances or the environment, somewhere along the line those figures of authority ... mama, papa, and whoever else that were their substitutes or cohorts ... got it across to us in clear and unmistakable terms that we hadn't made it. We

The Rest of Your Life

had not won their love. We had not won their approval. Of course this is based upon an old idea of theirs and that is that you earn approval. You have to perform to get it. It's not coming to you otherwise.

How clearly I remember that one of the most persistent things of my childhood, one of the first sentences that I remember, as a matter of fact was, "Be good Allen, or God won't love you!" Some years later I discovered that theologically, this is an absolute, falsehood. It was heresy. My mother and father and all the nuns and the priest could have been run out of the county for saying that ... with the Pope after them. But the harm had been done. I had gotten it clearly in my head that first I had to perform. And the basic need, the crying need of every human being is that they must matter of themselves. There must be worth, there must be love simply because they exist. Until you believe that, until you have found that, you have a search the rest of your life. And you use some of the strangest methods of trying to find it.

Now this idea is gotten over to you ... that you must perform ... by mama and dad, who are synonymous with God because they represent God ... because they are the giants of your childhood along with their aides that they employ such as teachers, brothers, sisters, nurses, aunts, uncles, and the law. How many of you were frightened with policemen when you were a kid? "If you don't behave, I'm going to call the police!"' the child tests this. He

What Are the Old Ideas?

says, "Well, I will perform. I will win their love." He tries in every way he knows. He tries first by using what he thinks is his definition of being good. But, since tie's dealing with neurotics or this would not happen, he's never good enough... never. He can't quite make it.

Another old idea was that the best way to keep discipline was to withhold approval, to withhold love. But no matter how well he performs, he can't get approval and right here we see the roots, the beginning of that thing that haunts the neurotic and the alcoholic ... that he must be better, he must be better. Two things are already being formed, the perfectionist complex and the aggressiveness.

There are a lot of books out today and one right now that's hit the best seller lists. The real theme of this book is that man's aggressiveness is instinctive and that he is a violent creature. But there is another opinion that has been around for a long time. It's not written as sensationally. It's written much more soundly. The anthropologists and sociologists who have done this work are much less spectacular and they don't make the bestseller lists. I was reading one of these books not long ago and I loved the way the author summarized his paper. With a beautiful paraphrase that was one of Shakespeare's great lines he says, "The fault lies not in our nature, but in our nurture." From my viewpoint I subscribe to this one hundred percent.

The Rest of Your Life

The *guilt*, the feeling of unworthiness now must be replaced with constant aggressiveness. "I must be better... I must be better... I must be better." Now these same parents , nuns, teachers... whoever they are in your background (I'm sorry I keep referring to mine, but then I know my background a little better than I know anyone else's), they too add to this because they are making up for their guilt. So you are in a way doing their work too.

I'm quite sure what my mother had in mind now that I look back knowing that she was very unhappy and very tormented and guilt-ridden woman, in spite of all her prayers and vigils, was to take us, her family, and hold us in her hand and make a burnt offering of us to God and say, "Look God...see what I've done? Here are all these plaster saints I have produced and they are yours and please now be easy on me." And of course, she lived to see her dreams go down in dust because we never made it. How could we? Mama's guilt could not be wiped out because it wasn't real. So nothing the kids ever did wiped it out.

We tried. I come from a long line of perfectionists and I come from a long line of competitors. The climate in which I was brought up in ... and I've found it again and again in other alcoholics I've talked to ... was not a climate of love, but one of competition, a climate of humiliation. We were always being compared to everyone else, not just with each other. I remember

What Are the Old Ideas?

thinking how I could plot to catch my brothers and sisters in sin. But I couldn't compete against the whole town and school. I could come home with straight A's right down the line. Then we would get to mathematics, where I was never to strong because I didn't like the nun who taught mathematics, and there would be a B. Mama looked at that B and those A's and then we had a big conference. It always ended up by her saying, "What did Daniel McKafferty get in mathematics? What did Patrick MacMahon get in mathematics?"

But long before he gets to this age, this little kid is testing whether or not he can perform, whether or not he can win them over, and of course he doesn't do it. So he begins to feel that there must be something wrong with him. That could be the only explanation. There's something wrong with him. He doesn't know that anybody else is going through this. He doesn't know it at all. He simply tests. He tries. Later on he is going to, as I did, alternate ... trying and not trying ... trying and not trying. It's why so many of us had this Dr. Jekyll and Mr. Hyde pattern of life. It's why so many of us subscribed to the old idea of *all or nothing at all*, because this was the only way we could live. How could you live with perfection minded figures of authority out of your childhood and then say, "Well, I'll just walk the middle road?" I remember one time in confession being told by a wise, wise priest who broke the seal of confession by calling me by my first name. I went so

The Rest of Your Life

often, he had no chance of not knowing who it was. "Allen, for you virtue lies in the middle road." And I thought, "Oh well, he's an old man and he doesn't know what he's talking about. How could virtue lie in the middle road? Virtue is excellence. Virtue is the summit. Virtue is the top."

Now, what could possibly come from all this guilt? Is this guilt just going to go along by itself all the time? Is the child going to be *mea culpaing* all his life? No. Pretty soon he has *anger*. The inevitable result of guilt and unworthiness is anger. Because, as I said, after he has tested it and has done everything he can think of, and he can't win ... it's always more, more, more ... he quits and says, "Well, I won't." Now he has to express this anger because anger doesn't go away. Guilt doesn't go away until we find out what's causing it. The first time he tries the anger, he finds out that he better never do it again because he is slapped back. This little tiny kid is put in his place not only physically, but with the cruelest kind of punishment of all ... the one that I referred to and one that's taught so good...the withholding of approval, the withholding of acceptance, the withholding of love.

So what is he going to do with this anger if he can't express it? He starts turning it in upon himself, and we have the beginning of a neurosis because, after all, that is what the neurotic pattern is. It is the pattern of self-destructive behavior; compulsive ... this drama that is being enacted over and over and over again.

What Are the Old Ideas?

He begins to do things that occur to him that he thinks he has found out in his childhood are the worst things he could possibly do. Even though the moralists named them for far different reasons centuries ago, they ended up being incredibly accurate. Because these secret sins, these secret transgressions that so haunt and torment the childhood of so many of us were under the all-inclusive term of self-abuse. And that's really what it was. It was anger turned in upon yourself, anger that increased the guilt, anger that could not be expressed any other way. And, of course, now the guilt is becoming logical and objective guilt because the child is doing things that he has been taught are wrong.

What can result now from *guilt and anger*? There's no place else to go ... *fear*! Fear is going to become the constant companion, the preferred companion really. These fears largely divide themselves into two groups: the fear of punishment and the fear of discovery. I hope that they rang as much of a bell with you as they did with me. When I finally said, "What in the hell am I really afraid of?" (I had been calling them things like impending doom. We all love that ... feeling of *impending doom*.) When I finally sat down and thought about it, I was afraid that I was going to be discovered. I was afraid that I was going to be punished and finally, I had to face the fear.

I said to myself, "All right, What if the Los Angeles Times came out tomorrow and the headlines, in type that hadn't

The Rest of Your Life

been used since Pearl Harbor, said, 'McGinnis Exposed! The True Facts About Allen Reid Francis Xavier McGinnis As Told To Otis Chandler!' What would I do?" It's the ultimate fear, the fear of discovery, and it matters a lot more than the fear of God when you get right down to it. Because you see, by the time I was about ten years old my announced objective in life ... the only real objective I had and hoped for in all my activity and in all my prayers and penances ... was just that I wanted to make it to purgatory. I figured that if I got there, that's about all I could ask for. That would be enough. Heaven? Who in hell is going to make it to Heaven? If I could just make it to purgatory. Now you stay there, of course, for eons! But that's all right. If I could just make it there As a matter of fact, I hated myself so much with this guilt ... these compulsive actions, I realize now...that when I came into AA and for many years afterwards, I felt that what might finally win me salvation, what might finally get me past the judgment, was the fact that a man who hated himself as much as I did could not be all bad. I thought this might do it.

Now we've talked about some old ideas. I touched on just a few because I think that this is the unholy trinity that tyrannizes us ... *Guilt, Anger, Fear.* Everything else comes out of them. But they have their little labyrinths and they have their little tributaries, and you will have to fill them in. When we ask, "Why doesn't one taking of the fourth step, one taking of the fifth step,

What Are the Old Ideas?

end these feelings?" It is because we are fighting cherished beliefs that we have held all our lives ...because we were taught them. We were taught them.

I put forth many, many reasons why my first go round at this Fellowship was a failure after the first three months ... when I resigned and went my way. All of the reasons that I have advanced are partially true. But really there was one main contributing thing all the time and that was the cherished belief ... the old idea that I had and came here with and never said, never breathed it to a soul ... and it was, "Well hell, what can this thing do for me? I have been a member of the one true church. I have been taught it; I have believed it and I have practiced it. Now if that couldn't keep me from drinking, what the hell is this man-made organization that started in Akron, Ohio, 14 years ago going to do for me?" That's why it was never real to me from the very beginning. I held onto that old idea.

I had to come to grips with the most basic beliefs I had. I had to come to grips with things that I had been saying all of my life. "All or nothing at all." If you want to be something, be it and you will gradually become it!" You don't really become what you're practicing. A man always ends up being what he thinks he is way down deep. This always betrays him. This is the sad thing about how we try to compensate for this guilt and this fear and this

The Rest of Your Life

anger because we all take the same course. I've never found anybody who didn't do it.

We adopt a two-way technique that keeps wiping us out. On the one hand we have this bottomless tyrannical, insatiable need for approval because, since we hate ourselves, there has got to be this instant universal approval from everybody. And the tragic thing about this is how it betrays us ... satisfying this need. How we lie! How we fawn! How we flatter! The times that we compromise everything we believe, in order to have the approval, and then we wipe it all out with the same people we're trying to win over ... because we are so afraid of them and because we are so sure that we will, one day, be discovered ... by trying to cut them down ... trying to keep them under control. We have this need to humiliate, this need to retaliate, this need to dominate, this need to excel. And of course, we are smiled upon through all of this neurotic activity because it is the activity of our society. It is the favored method of our culture and our environment. Maybe today's generation is going to discover (and maybe they have already started) that this has got to go. Some of the old ideas have got to go.

The old ideas and how do you let go of them? In the next session I hope to put forth some suggestions for you of how you go about this ... how you might try be- ginning to go about letting go of these things. But I would like you to keep one thing in

What Are the Old Ideas?

your mind. Let's go back to a statement ... we might even be bold enough to call it a revelation ... of St. John's; in the book of John, when God said, "You will know the truth and the truth will make you free!" Nobody has ever quarreled with that and it's been around in other words before the book of John. Try to remember this. The real enemies of the truth are not too often the lies ... the deliberate, committed, dishonest lies...but rather the myths. The myths that are so persistent and so persuasive because they are so unrealistic. Far too often in our lives, we cling to the clichés of our forefathers. We cling to the clichés that were handed to us. We subject all of the facts that we have right in front of us to a prefabricated set of interpretations and we end up enjoying, while we are dying, the comfort of opinion without the discomfort of thought.

Question and Answer Period

Why do I have this feeling of not belonging even when I try, and take part as much as I can? ... I am new.

I've been talking about that. The feeling of not belonging is based on this subjective guilt, this feeling of unworthiness... this feeling that you will be discovered. Why do you suppose that we have kept this wall up all our lives? It's the fear of discovery. The fear that someone else will find out and share the opinion that we have of ourselves. It's too bad that we sometimes don't trust the opinions of others because they are, in nearly every instance, more charitable to us than we are to ourselves.

What Are the Old Ideas?

I told a lie to obtain money for drugs. The lie was that I said my wife and son got killed in an accident. How will I ever make amends for that?

I don't think you should worry about that. A person who is in the grip of a physical need for drugs can hardly be held morally responsible and I would forget about it. The fact that you have written it now shows that you realize that you did something that is making you feel terribly, terribly guilty. We have all done these things. There are things in my life that have never shown up on an inventory because they were not morally wrong and there was nothing about them that I would need to tell anybody. But I've gotten around to where I tell them because it frees me.

I remember one of the things that bugged me for a number of years. I was driving down the street and I did something wrong. I cut in front of this guy and he called me a son-of-a bitch. Right away I reacted. I cut him off and stopped the car. I jumped out of my car and went over to his and said, "You called me a son-of-a-bitch and no man calls me a son-of-a-bitch." He got out of his car and I looked up ... and up ... and l backed away and talked my way out of it and said, "Well, there's no reason for us to lose our temper." I got in my car and I was sick ... sick to my stomach at what I had done. That has never shown up on an inventory, but a

The Rest of Your Life

lot of times when I was drunk, I remembered it and sometimes now, the memory will come back and I actually get k. Why? Because I was a coward ... I was a coward. As a matter of fact, most of the fighting I've done all my life was to prove that I wasn't afraid and I never proved it to myself. *Having been brainwashed by nuns and priests,* (they're just catching hell, aren't they?) *could you give some suggestions on how to take the third step*? Yes. I'll tell you what was once told to me and it was a great thing. It was told to me on a retreat. That was another thing I did. I discovered retreats. I tried everything. I would go on retreats thinking, surely, that if I could keep my mouth shut for three days, I could expect a miracle for it. I was pouring out what I was always pouring out ... my self-hatred, my self-condemnation, and this priest said to me, "Do you believe that God is love?" And I said, "Yes, that's the definition. I believe that God is love." Then he said, "Do you believe that He has shown some Interest in you and your life? You have been baptized into a religion you were brought up in and you believe in God. Would you then say, Allen, that God has shown some interest in you?" I said, "Yes. I believe that He is intensely interested in me ... intensely interested in me. I just wish that I was worthy of Him." And then he said this. "Then if God is love, it follows as the night to day that He could not be interested in anything that is not lovable." If you can meditate on that, you can take the third step.

What Are the Old Ideas?

Is it not necessary, as you acquire more honesty in working the Program, for you to take more than one fourth and fifth steps?

What I have been talking about is a continuation of the fourth and fifth steps, but I'm glad that question was asked because I want to bring this out and I want to emphasize it. Once you have taken it from a moral viewpoint ... from the standpoint of accusing yourself of moral wrong ... once you have done that, I don't think that you should ever do it again because I don't think there is any need for it. I think that even though you remember things that you forgot the first time around, there will come an occasion where you can tell it. There will be a right occasion. Maybe when you're doing 12th step work or trying to help somebody else then you can tell something that you forgot. But don't, for God's sake, keep picking at the sores of your past. This is the most destructive pastime that you can indulge in and I know you will want to do it because again this comes from this need for perfection ... this need to go over it and over it and over it. From now on, as the therapy of AA progresses, try to take it from the stand- point of what was the motivation behind the behavior? Quit thinking of it as right or wrong. What was it and what were you after? What was behind it and what was the result? Besides, the tenth step takes care of the day- to day

The Rest of Your Life

.   Please discuss depression after a year's sobriety or more. I think all of the things I have been talking about are answers to that question. Depression, discouragement ... these things come from the subjective feelings of guilt ... the anger ... the suppressed anger ... the fear. When you realize this and begin to trace back again and again and again, and it's going to take time to see what you were after and sometimes it requires help. Somebody has to help you to do this ... to see what you were doing when you were performing these patterns of behavior. The guilt begins to go because you were not out to offend God. You were not out to throw society into a garbage heap. What you were really doing was trying to survive ... trying to get through one day after another while you were consumed with this guilt and fear and anger. All these neurotic patterns were techniques of survival and you couldn't blame a man if he's swimming to shore, trying to save his life, if he swims in a way that the Olympic coach might not approve of. He's got to get there. And this is what we did. And one day, when you understand this enough that the self-condemnation begins to go ... when a certain amount of self-acceptance comes and self-acceptance always leads to self-approval ... you find that you can make a choice. You can say to yourself, "Do I want to keep doing this or don't I? Do I have to follow this neurotic pattern or don't I? I know what I was after, now what was I trying to do? Do I want to keep getting what I'm getting and pay the price for it or don't I?"

What Are the Old Ideas?

I've heard many referrals to the moral viewpoint and the moral inventory. In taking my personal inventory, should I use my moral code or maybe a more conservative one?

I know exactly what you mean and I'm laughing because I think you're having such a dilemma. It doesn't have to be one way or the other. When you take it, why don't you take it from both viewpoints? You can see how you feel and whatever the conservative viewpoint is. As long as whatever you've done has been done honestly or to the degree of honesty you are capable of on that particular day, and you don't have to worry about what that degree is ... you just do it. I think that the first time around it's so simple really, you say, "I did this. I was taught that it was very, very wrong. I don't feel that way now but this is what I did." You see, there's no problem. That's just the way you do it.

If neurotic parents create the future neurotic, how can you try not to be a neurotic parent?

Well, your children are growing up. You will grow up with them. The McGinnis' would have come out fine and dandy if this had taken place in our family; if the whole family had come along in the same way. What we needed in that family was love. We needed

The Rest of Your Life

to love each other. No matter what we did to each other, we needed there to be understanding and willingness to try together. Understanding that there was to be no punishment, no constant withholding of approval, no competition. That we were going to make our mistakes together and we were going to see it through together. But we never did it that way. There was a goal, always a goal, held in front of us that was unreachable and nobody got there. And you, starting out, can gather those children around you. You are going to grow with them and, as you grow, they will grow right along with you and one day, their children will be a credit to you for what you're doing now.

What do you do when the husband is very neurotic and makes demands on the children?

Are you an alcoholic? (*Yes.*) And he's a nonalcoholic? (*Yes.*) Have you suggested that he go to Alanon? (*He goes once a week.*) Well, he's doing what he can. The therapy has started. I doubt if he's the only perfectionist in the family though. You're laughing, okay, well now you're getting better.

What I'm trying to do and I seek your approval, is to work the Program of attraction because the only person that I can change is me and I'm trying to be the best damn me I can and I the kid wants

What Are the Old Ideas?

a piece of the action, he can climb on board and that's the best I can do. I can't seem to make him do what I want. Right?

No, don't. That's what we have been talking about. Don't put on your children the burden of winning your place in society or with God or anywhere else.

Isn't depression a normal course of living?

I don't know how to answer this question about depression because, apparently, it means a great many things to different people. I was told by those who were supposed to know that all my life I had a great deal of emotional resiliency. I plunged to the depths, but apparently I plunged so hard and so fast I always bounced. So, my depressions were short lived. I found out though that when I went around saying I was depressed, when I really went back to what triggered it, somebody had always hurt my feelings. Somebody had always made me feel not loved and I wasn't appreciated and by God, other people were getting the recognition due to me. So I was depressed. Now that's the way it was with me. It was a stirring up of the old guilt. A triggering of the old guilt. The little boy that couldn't win the approval. The little boy that couldn't be number one. And this was the way it was all my life. I said once that I had a very simple technique of

The Rest of Your Life

behavior. I was always jumping up in your lap to be petted and if you didn't pet me, I jumped off your lap and I bit you. And generally, when you jump off the lap and bite people, you are in a depression.

The Neurotic Nine!

Session 4
July 25, 1968

The Rest of Your Life

The Neurotic Nine!

IT'S ALWAYS a drag to try to get through these preliminaries, but they have to be gotten through so that we all get on the same wavelength. Number one, I want to remind you of this again and again because there's nothing more important in AA to be reminded of that neither I nor any other member of this Fellowship speaks officially for Alcoholics Anonymous. We hear very often the book ALCOHOLICS ANONYMOUS referred to as our "only authority," but that "only authority" constantly reminds you that it is meant to be suggestive only. What I'm doing up here is what every other member of this fellowship tries to do and that is to share my opinions, my convictions, my beliefs based upon my experience, with you. They are my opinions. They can be held against me but not against AA. If you keep that in mind, then

The Rest of Your Life

nothing I say up here need distress you at all. So please, always remember that that is the premise upon which any member of AA speaks to you whether he remembers to tell you that or not. Number two, if you are a beginner and what I start talking to you about here tonight brings to your mind a question that sounds something like, "What in the hell is he talking about? I came here to learn how to stop drinking." all you need to be told tonight or in any other meeting for a long, long time, is that you don't have to listen to any of this if you don't want to. If you're a newcomer, all you have to do is stay away from the first drink. And you're going to ask how that's done. That is done in one way and one way only. You don't take any booze through your mouth or any other opening that I know of. The only motivation that you can have for this that makes any sense at all is that you value being sober more than you value being drunk and we can't give that motivation to you. That has to come from inside. But that's all you have to keep in mind. That's the only way any of us ever stayed sober. We did not come here and find a pill or some exercise or a diet of leafy green vegetables that helped us stay sober. We found out that we had to take the first step. We had to admit that we were alcoholics and we had to decide in our own minds whether or not we valued sobriety. And when I define sobriety, I mean the absence from the bloodstream of booze or any other chemical that will change your thinking.

The Neurotic Nine!

What we started here the first Thursday of this month was what I like to refer to as a workshop on alcoholism. We tried to keep a theme going by asking ourselves certain questions, and I won't get where I want to get if I try to review each one of them so I'm only going to review where we left off last week. We asked ourselves the question, "What are the old ideas?" that we heard about in the book. In the third paragraph of chapter five that you hear read in Southern California at all AA meetings, one of the most significant statements in the book, I believe, says, "Some of us have tried to hold on to our old ideas and the result was nil until we let go absolutely."[4] So we tried to define what are the old ideas because we found out we had to do it.

We had, in previous weeks, gone through the first, the second, the third, fourth and fifth steps. We had taken our inventory as well as we knew how. We had activated this by admitting to God, to ourselves and to another human being, the exact nature of our wrongs. And we found that it was a calming experience, but, to everyone, after the initial euphoria and practically a shedding of weight that takes place when this is done, the old drives, the old fears, the old neuroses, the old self-recriminations, the old troubles return little by little by little. So, last week, in working this out, we found that what really happened with these old ideas that started way, way back in childhood, was

---

[4] Page 58, ALCOHOLICS ANONYMOUS

The Rest of Your Life

that we were really being motivated by an unholy trinity of, first, *guilt*. A subjective guilt that came from a feeling of unworthiness that had been passed on to us by our parents and the other giants of our childhood who shaped and molded our childhood. A feeling that we had failed to win the approval and the love to which we felt we were entitled and the reason that we had failed was because it was our fault. There was something either missing in us or we were doing something wrong.

When this guilt got to us pretty good, we tried to express it. We tried to test whether or not we could do anything about it because it aroused in us a great resentment and a great *anger*. We tried to express this anger because anger will not go away. Something has to be done about it or it finds an outlet even though it wears a thousand masks. We found that the child can't express his anger because he's not big enough. He can't get away with it. Pigmies don't win battles with giants and he is surrounded by giants. Since anger won't go away, he found out that what he really begins to do very, very early as a child is to mask the anger. He tries to express it in different ways but mainly he turns it in upon himself, chiefly because he does feel guilty because he feels that he has failed; because he feels that he is an unworthy person in his own right. And, to make the subjective guilt which he has been haunted by real, he begins to rebel. He begins to be a bad boy, a bad girl. He begins to sin secret sins. He makes this guilt in his

The Neurotic Nine!

mind real because he can't forgive himself for having incurred this guilt and he serves his anger. And now these two beget the final thing ... *fear* ... which grows and grows and grows and is mainly of two varieties; the fear of punishment and the fear of discovery...the fear of being found out.

Now that's where we left off last week. This is going to be the soil in which the future alcoholic, the future neurotic, and I'd like you, if you would, to use those terms interchangeably in your mind ... this is where it all begins and accompanies him for the rest of his life as he begins to find out what's going on. Since we tell you that it is the opinion of AA, by most of us, that alcoholism is a symptom of deeper troubles, then this is what motivates the ability to be able to face life on its terms without the aid of booze.

At this time the child, having been nurtured on these three tyrants ... *guilt, anger and fear* ... has got to devise some kind of survival plan. I think that even the little child sits back, stands back, and gives the world a long, long look and carefully divides it into two groups: those who hate him and those who don't like him. Now, they are the enemy. They become *they* and he feels, always of course, that he didn't make them the enemy. Something about him caused them to be the enemy. That he is unworthy, he is guilty, but he must try to hide this and he must not let them know how angry he is at them and how angry, mainly, he is at himself.

The Rest of Your Life

So, when you have two groups, those who hate you and those who don't like you, you're going to have to have some kind of a way to survive and generally, classically, all neurotics start out about it the same way. They play two games. One game might be called, "If I can make them love me, they won't hurt me." This is the game that calls for the seeking for approval, the seeking for admiration, for acceptance, for getting instantaneous, universal love from the world. Now even a little kid knows in his little tiny childish mind (he's been around long enough) that he's not really going to get all his enemies to love him, even though he's never going to give up trying.

But there's no use having this one plan of attack. He balances this with another game and this game might be called, "If I am stronger than they are, then they can't hurt me." So he's got himself protected both ways. He's hedging his bet. This is where he comes in and he's got all the blessings of society for this. He now competes. He is going to keep on proving that mama and dad were wrong. He is really the best. He is really worthy of love and admiration and he's going to show all these giants that they were wrong because he's going to be better than they are, stronger than they are, which is where the sense of guilt came from in the first place by his always being told he wasn't.

Now all this has very acceptable names in our environment, in our culture, in our society. It's called competing,

The Neurotic Nine!

being in the honor group, being in the top ten, etcetera, etcetera, and etcetera. Well you see, that's the trouble. There's only room for ten at the top and there's more. There's more than ten and then the one who is number one ... there are nine behind him and he's not sure that all nine of them shouldn't be ahead of him. So it gets very, very mixed up.

This is the plan of survival that the neurotic, the future alcoholic embarks on. It's obvious that he's going to have to put together some pretty good tools and have some pretty good strategy so he puts together what you might call a little do-it-yourself *survival kit*. He calls it a survival kit because he thinks that's what it is. He looks upon these things as escape routes. This is the way he keeps distance. This is the way he keeps alive. This is the way he keeps breathing room. This is the way he keeps everybody from finding out and destroying him. In reality what it is, is a do-it-yourself *torture kit.* All of this is, as we hope we call examine and see that the ultimate result of the two drives: the drive for approval and the drive to dominate ... the drive to get people to love you and the drive to get people to fear you ... is that they wipe each other out constantly. This is why there is such a Dr. Jekyll and Mr. Hyde pattern to the lives of most neurotics and most alcoholics.

Now, what are some of the, shall we call them tools, in our survival kit? What are some of the common things by which

The Rest of Your Life

people implement this plan ... this double-barreled technique of being loved and feared in the same breath because that is exactly what the neurotic wants? He wants to be loved. He wants tears to come into the eyes of people as they behold him, and at the same time that they are shaking with love for him, they are to shake with fear of him. Their knees are to be knocking because they don't dare offend him. There can only be rose petals dropped in his path while he is, of course, secretly convinced that he should be shot down in the sun like a dog. Here are some tools I made up in my mind this afternoon ... a list of mile. There's probably a lot more but these time came to me because they were all in my little do-it-yourself kit. I will not name them in any particular order. I have my ideas but you can put them in whatever order you want to.

I'm going to start with one that might surprise you and that is *Religion*. I've heard a statement over the years that has reverberated from the walls of AA meetings. Probably you will hear it less as time goes by, I don't know. I still hear it from the podium again and again and the statement goes, "I tried religion and it failed." This would lead me to believe that: (a) most of the people who come into AA have some kind of religious background that is still sitting in their minds a lot more than they ever cared to admit; and (b) it also leads me to believe that this must have been a very important tool in the survival kit as it was with me.

The Neurotic Nine!

I can only speak about the Christian religion because that is the one into which I was born and in which I was raised. There is a great thing that I read once and it was this, "Christianity has not really failed; it has just not ever been tried." I think that I agree with this. Please believe me and understand that my remarks here tonight are in no way in criticism of your religion, my religion, or anybody else's religion. What I'm talking about is how it becomes adapted as a tool in the torture kit because of the way it is presented to the child. And I'm afraid that this comes about because, all too often, religion and God are being submitted and presented to the child by the figures of authority who represent Him and with whom He is forever going to be identified in the child's mind.

God is presented, not as a support, not as a refuge, not as a haven, and not as somebody that will accept you in your own right. He is more or less submitted as an arbiter, a judge, a code, and a scorer. A lot of times he's nothing more than a glorified teller in a bank. And religion becomes an inaccessible frame of reference; a standard of performance that we're never going to achieve so that, in our self-flagellation, self-destruction torture kit, we can constantly keep going around saying, "I can't do it ... I tried, but He doesn't listen to me ... who am I to ask God?...Mea Culpa...Mea Culpa." You know, get out the prayers, get out the abstinence, and get out *all* the things. Let's drape the church in

The Rest of Your Life

black because this penitent soul is not really ever going to make it. In the beautiful story in the Bible, the prodigal son comes home and it is assumed that he stays. I was always coming and leaving. I played it in serial fashion because every time I got back I thought, "I don't really belong here ... he doesn't really like me ... I'll never make it so it's on to the corn husks again." Religion is one of the tools. Let's move on to another one.

It's obvious that the neurotic, in his survival, is going to have to have some multi-purpose weapons... weapons that can serve a lot of purposes and be adaptable to a lot of uses. Let's take one of the tools that brought you here...*Booze*. You keep the word booze in your mind and let's see how multi-purpose it is. As you think about booze and all the different circumstances and environments in which you used it, let's go down the list of some of the needs that we experienced over the years and how we expressed them. The need to celebrate; the need to rebel; the need to relax; the need to dominate; the need for bravery; the need for stimulation; the need to express anger; the need to find the courage; the need to blot out remorse; the need to get up the nerve to do what we didn't have the nerve to do sober; the need to forget that we got drunk to do what we couldn't do sober ... we begin to see that booze is a very multi-purpose tool.

Now let's try another tool that we used the same way. Let's take that wonderful three-letter word ... *Sex*. You're going to

The Neurotic Nine!

say, "Sex is a multi-purpose tool in the survival kit or the torture kit? You mean sex can be a neurotic implement," Okay, then let's take a similar list of needs ... the need for admiration; the need for approval; the need for acceptance; the need to dominate; the need to humiliate; the need to degrade; the need to withhold; the need to punish? Does this little three-letter word fit? I was talking the other day to a guy along these lines who said to me, "Allen, everything you say is making very great sense but I certainly never used sex as a means of winning approval. With me it was a forth right thing that I enjoyed." And I said, "Buster, you mean to tell me that you have never recited the lover's litany?" He said, "What's that?" I said, "You have never heard coming out of your mouth, at certain moments. 'Do you love me? Am I the best? How did I measure up? Am I all right? How do I rank?' You mean you've never heard this?" Let's go on to another one. I think we've dwelt there long enough.

We come now to one that I call, because it's a personification, the *Critic*. I'm sure you've all known people like this but I'm quite sure that you probably don't recognize it in yourself. Maybe you do. There are a lot of medical men and psychiatrists and psychologists who have made a study of alcoholism over the years and they seem to think that hypercriticism, a hypercritical attitude towards everybody around you, is unfailingly present in the makeup of every alcoholic.

The Rest of Your Life

Besides the critic's methodology being an implement of escape, the tool that he uses is humiliation. He uses humiliation because that is what was used against him as a child. This is where the punishment and really where the anger started. It was not so much the physical punishment but the withholding of love; the withholding of approval; the being told that we didn't measure up. As a matter of fact, after seventy years of clinical experience, the world's philosophers and psychiatrists that followed this are almost unanimously agreed that modern man's greatest fear is the fear of being made a fool of. This has long since replaced the fear-of-death; the fear of plague; the fear of increase; the fear of not being survived by children ...all these ancient fears. Modern man's fear is the fear of being humiliated and we use this against each other and we use it against ourselves. The critic...the nagger ... you find this tool used at its full flower, I believe, and I don't mean to take sides here, but I think you really find it in its finest expression in the female gender. I told you that you didn't have to agree with me.

Let's take another tool that is very common in both sexes and flowers in both very, very well. It reaches full bloom. It is *Self-pity* and *Martyrdom*. This is the game where we use a lot of pronouns, but we never use the pronoun I. We use the pronouns he, him, her, they, them. They're the ones. I didn't do it, I've been here all the time, world, trying my best; trying to do what I could, would, and all the while *you've* been out there plotting. And who

The Neurotic Nine!

wouldn't get drunk; who wouldn't leap from motel to motel; who wouldn't rebel against God the way *they* are; those tigers and those other things that are out there? Carried to an extreme this is known as paranoia. So be careful if you are convinced that when two people are whispering, they are talking about you. I could be in a room where there was a big crowd and it would be hard to see me because I'm not very tall, but I could see two people over in the corner talking and I felt sure that they were talking about me. I wasn't sure that they could even see me but I knew they were discussing me and I knew what they were saying.

Another game is the game of *Withdrawal*. There is another phase you hear in AA, over and over. I'm a *loner*. Why are we all loners? We get a look like a cocker spaniel. We're special, very special and we're loners. We have all kinds of euphemisms for this and, oh God, how I've used them over the years. I always went around saying that I always felt *apart from...* I've heard this many, many times on the lips of other people. I know I was giving myself a break by using a very euphemistic expression for what I really felt and that was I felt I was *unacceptable to*, not *apart from*. I was *unacceptable to*. Now, how do you keep people from finding out that you are unacceptable to them? You stay apart from them. This way they are in the wrong and they don't find out anything about you. Withdrawal.

The Rest of Your Life

As we go through these, try to refer them back to those three things ... the guilt, the anger, and the fear. See how they are inextricably intertwined. I think that this loner business is nothing at all but this guilt, this feeling of unworthiness, this feeling that we really do not matter in our own right...that we have no importance of our own. We have no self-approval, we have no self-esteem and we do not want this found out. Therefore we have to be a loner. We have to be apart from. We cannot risk being vulnerable. We cannot risk being found that we are anything less than perfect.

The next has really become a worry and one of the great clichés in AA, I really believe. It's funny how the newcomer picks them up. Long before the newcomer is able to pronounce the word anonymous, he is telling you about his *Resentments.* And we hear, "How do I get rid of resentments?" Again we've come to this magic formula that must be found. When I came in and took my inventory, on about the fifth day because I had read the book and been to a couple of meetings ... which I felt I could improve on and there was no use wasting any time about this ... there was no word resentment. I thought, "Isn't that odd? It says here in the book that resentments are a luxury the alcoholic cannot afford, and hell, I don't even have this luxury. I don't even have this luxury to give up. God, I'm poorer than I thought. I don't have any resentments." I resented myself, which was perfectly clear to me then. The

The Neurotic Nine!

number one person that I didn't like was me, but I didn't think I didn't like anybody else. Well, the fact of the matter is that if I had started to make a list of the people I resented, it would have been endless. I never would have gotten through the inventory because, if we did that, then we could have started with God, worked through Adam and Eve on down. Finally we would end up with my boss and a few others that were inhabiting my world and spoiling my Garden of Eden at that moment. Why was I so blind? But, on the other hand, why did so many other people pick it up and say, right away ... I have resentments? I think it's because it expresses itself in different ways. I didn't realize then what I have come to believe; that an indispensible ingredient to forming resentment is that a person must pose some kind of a threat to you. Now when I use the word threat, it might bring the wrong images to mind, and yet, I don't know any other word to use. What I mean by posing a threat to you is that this person stands there as a...well, again I come back to this word ... threat. Let's try some other words. Now in envy, the person poses a threat because the person has something you want, so they threaten your security, they threaten your opinion of yourself. They threaten your being successfully able to conceal from the world the fact that you do not have what this other person has. Jealousy is the same way. The person is posing a threat. Maybe it will make it clearer if I say this: you never resent someone who is unimportant to you. It is always

The Rest of Your Life

someone who matters a great deal. That person can harm you in some way ... by withdrawing from you, by punishing you, by denying you in some way ... denying you their friendship, denying you their love, withdrawing from you, punishing you.

I don't believe that you can pray away resentments. I don't think you can smile them away. I don't think you can go along saying things like "it's really not the person, it's the principle of the thing, you know." You just make these speeches and inside of you, you know how hollow they are. I think you have to face it head on. Why is this person so important to you? Then deal with it on that basis and in a way that we'll get around to discussing next week.

There is another tool that is not often recognized, but it plays a very great role and ties back to religion. It ties back to a lot of things. In other words, it has different phrases and I'll try to bring it to you in a fresh way ... a different way of saying it tonight and see if the way I say it makes it any clearer. I call it the *Neurotic Need for Infallibility*. We talk about the same thing when we talk about perfection complex. It works in many, many ways, but it again comes back to this original guilt, fear, and anger when I learned, way back as a tiny kid, that I, of myself, have no worth that I, of myself, cannot win any kind of approval. So somewhere I must find some kind of perfect, perfect answer. Somewhere in the world there must exist something in which there is no flaw because

The Neurotic Nine!

this *something* becomes security for me. This *something* represents salvation. This is my magic talisman and this is the thing I am going to win through with in the end. A lot of times it's religion. A lot of times it's a person. A lot of times it's AA. We come in here and this *something* is thing that's been found; therefore, there must be no criticism of it. Just as when I came into AA I felt there must be no criticism of my religion. You must not find a flaw in it because it would destroy my security. It would destroy my security. Then I found that other people had the same attitude towards psychiatry or whatever ... name it ... whether it's free love, hippies, pot, LSD, name it ... somebody is trying it out because they think it is the perfect answer. It is going to be the solution. It is going to have no flaws. And you know what the perfect answer is ... the final security? If you live long enough, work long enough, face this hard enough, you find out that there is no perfect answer. Everything on the earth comes to you through creatures, and creatures are not perfect. So, there is no perfect organization, no perfect formula. There is no perfect man, no perfect woman, no perfect therapy, and no perfect anything. Your final security lies in trying to do what you can with what you have and with what you are.

This leads us to the last one. All along, what we've been talking about is a human being who is living his life based on the fact that he's right. The little, tiny child who embarked against

The Rest of Your Life

this giant enemy ... the two groups ... those who hate him and those who don't like him. He's been living his life on the defensive, and if you live your entire life on the defensive, it follows as the night to day, that you must have something to defend against. If you don't, you are out of business. With all of your torture kit ... all of your survival kit...you're not going to make it because nobody is pushing you around and the only thing you know how to do is defend ... defend. This is how you are surviving. Of course, it is how you are dying, but you think it is how you are surviving and so, there comes this *Need for Crisis*. The neurotic need for a crisis. If things are going well, my God, we're going to die. All is going to be lost. What do we do with the torture kit? What do we do with this thing? There goes my self-pity. Where is my martyrdom and where are my resentments? How am I going to live? There are no crises, so we make them. We write the script and we play it over and over. When you get right down to it, one of the best definitions of a neurosis is the fact that you are enacting a childhood drama over and over and over again. You write the same script. It's like the TV serial, Tarzan or some other, but what you do is you change the name and you change the locale and you change the cast of characters ... but, it's always either the water hole, or the barbed wire, or the guy who doesn't want to draw his gun anymore. And we play the script over and over and over again. In enacting the drama, if there's no crisis around, you make one. We'll talk next

108

The Neurotic Nine!

week about how to counteract that with a much more constructive game.

The need for a crisis. Some months ago, I sat down with a guy that was literally going out of his mind. He was crawling the wall and we went down the list one by one. He'd done a lot of work so it wasn't difficult. Finally, I looked at him and said, "You know what's going on, I believe?" And he said, "What's that?" I said, "You don't have a crisis. Nothing is wrong with your life, so you are here, rending your garments and saying, 'Allen, what should I do? Where am I sick? Where have I failed? ... What did you do when you felt like this?'" I did the same thing. I went out and screwed things up again so I could get in there and straighten them out. I've got to get in there. I've got to take care of it, you know, and you carry this to ridiculous extremes. For years I hired people who were inferior to me. I didn't know that I was doing that. I kept running around saying that you couldn't find any good writers; that you couldn't find any good art directors, goddammit, and I don't know what's happening today ... there's no talent around ... all they want is money. I was unconsciously but deliberately hiring people so that we wouldn't have good work so that I could come along and blame them and fix it up and say, "Well, I did it again." And they would go home saying, "They don't appreciate me and they don't pay me enough."

We've got ten minutes for questions.

The Rest of Your Life

Question and Answer Period

Do you have any pointers on taking the fourth step?

I've read guides on how to take the fourth step. I have read outlines, suggested outlines, and I have read what it says in the book. All of them have a great deal to offer but I think the simplest thing to do, the first time around, and I see it brings good results with practically everybody who has ever tried this, is to just sit down and write. Sit down and try to tell yourself the story of your life in plain unvarnished terms. Tell the good things that happened to you, and the bad things, and what you did ... always covering those things that made you feel guilty, that made you feel ashamed, that made you feel that you wanted to run away and die. Take your

The Neurotic Nine!

time and do it as honestly as you can. Of course, as your state of sobriety lengthens, more and more will be revealed to you ... no matter ... this is part of the growing therapy of AA and you don't need to be upset about this. When you have finished this, I think you will have a perspective on your life as an event, and as a pattern of behavior, that you never had before because you kept dismissing yourself, as we all were prone to do by saying, as one man told me, "My inventory was very simple. I wrote one sentence. I am a no good son-of-a-bitch."

You've talked about anger and guilt and fear. What do you do about uncontrollable anger? What causes it?

You mean the sudden welling up of uncontrollable anger? Something triggers an over-reaction and your defenses go. What has been repressed for years and years and is still largely repressed comes bubbling up like a volcano. Some little tiny thing happens and there's an uncontrollable anger and it's this ancient, ancient anger that has been diverted back. It has been expressed another way and it comes up this time as the real thing, anger, and it frightens you because you think you have lost control. I found that if you can keep from hurting anybody, it helps. I generally managed to do this because, nearly every time this happened to me, I was in the presence of people who were bigger than me.

The Rest of Your Life

Sometimes I didn't, and I hurt people. Sometimes I lashed out. This is a very common thing. Anger does not go away. It has to either be understood or expressed or it will be masked ... pushed down ... and come up in some other way.

How does a newcomer go about picking the right sponsor?

I didn't pick a sponsor, they got me. Two of them did and they never let me out of their sight. I would choose somebody whose approach toward AA, towards survival, and towards life, is one I admired. I would go up to them and say, "Would you mind helping me see if we can work out a relationship that would lead to your being my sponsor?" That's what I would do.

What do you do about an overwhelming amount of remorse and guilt that brings on depression?

Were you here last week when we talked about guilt? Remorse is this bitter disappointment again. The child's bitter disappointment and he's flagellating himself all over again as an adult. He's got a great way of rationalizing everything from the Ten Commandments to the latest decision of the Supreme Court. It's this old disappointment at not winning approval, at not being loved for yourself alone. It comes from thinking that your worth is based upon your performance and therefore, if your performance falls,

The Neurotic Nine!

you're going to be tormented by feelings of guilt. This is why we try to understand that this began with a subjective guilt that had nothing to do with performance. It was passed on to you as a legacy and that's what brings on this depression. It is a false standard ... a false frame of reference that we have carried with us all these years. Did we feel that our worth in God's eyes and in the eyes of the world was constantly based upon our performance and therefore, if we're going to have any worth, our performance had to be without flaw?

This belief, brought from the past, is an illusion, an unreal thing, and we will talk about this and see that it is a neurosis. We will drop phrases like "the best of my ability," and this constant bringing up of this neurotic frame of reference, this neurotic goal of measuring everything against it. We want to fail. Failing is part of the kit that we've been talking about here. We think that we're on escape routes. We say that we are trying to survive when what we are trying to do is fail. We are defending against intolerable fear, intolerable guilt, and intolerable anxiety by punishing ourselves. We are embarked on a self-destruct course. It's in the turning this around and seeing that the survival kit is, in truth, a destruction kit that we then have a whole new frame of reference and a whole new way of functioning.

The Rest of Your Life

Isn't the old reaction in uncontrollable anger also uncontrollable anxiety ... fear ... the triggering of an old reaction?

Anger is always the result of fear but I wouldn't call fear anger or anger fear. When they come along, you can recognize them.

Allen, in your opinion, is it possible to achieve any of these goals while still under the influence of alcohol, drugs, or pot?

No ... no. I think this is why we come to AA in a chorus saying ... I tried religion and it failed. I tried medicine, and it failed. I tried all those things and you tried all those things and they failed because, not only were we playing these games and working this torture kit all the time, but we were also muddying up the whole process by getting this head more dumb-dumb than it already was. Once you do sober up and try to begin to do all this, I believe that everybody has found that all these things have been very helpful retroactively ... anything that they have done. There were circumstances in my case that every day in AA and in every day of my sobriety, I drew on things that I had done before but, as I have said, they had not worked.

The Neurotic Nine!

A friend of 18 years stopped by and he was stoned out of his skull and I made a great discovery. I am 34 days sober and these drunks ... they're slobs and they smell ... and he couldn't leave soon enough for me. Then, later on this week, I began to think ... is this wrong of me to toss him aside so easily? I mean, after 18 years of friendship?

Did he ask you for help?

Well, he was very curious.

Did he ask you for help?

He asked if I had a drink.   That's that man's idea of help.

Did you give it to him?

No. I didn't have one.

Well, you see, you failed him. I guess that's all.

The Rest of Your Life

After the Old Ideas, What?

Session 5

August 1, 1968

The Rest of Your Life

After the Old Ideas, What?

I DIDN'T THINK it would ever get here, but it did. This is the wrap-up and to those of you faithful, hardy souls who stayed all through, I'm going to try and make it all add up to something tonight. First, let me remind you please, that anything you hear tonight from this position is my opinion and my opinion only. No one speaks officially for Alcoholics Anonymous. Second, I saw a lot of hands go up of newcomers. I hope that most of you have been here during these past weeks. But, to bring us up-to-date because there's a lot of ground to cover, let's review briefly so we're all going in the same direction and will end tip at the same place.

The Rest of Your Life

You'll recall that when I started this five weeks ago, I talked about seeing that your own house was in order so that great events could come to pass for you and countless others. And we set out to see if we could build such a house for ourselves; one in which we could live, and if it could be built sturdily enough, soundly enough, and have enough warmth and hospitality in it, that maybe someday we could invite others to share it. We could help them find there the shelter that we had had to ask from others who went before us. And we started out by asking ourselves a series of questions.

The number one question of that first meeting and its answer is, in my opinion, the fundamental requirement for recovery from alcoholism. It's the basis without which there is nothing else. "What is the point of sobriety?" You remember we examined this at length with the conclusion that if you're an alcoholic, the point of sobriety is life itself. It is assumed that if you have made a decision to stay sober, being an alcoholic, that you have chosen life rather than death. And since for you and for me sobriety is an indispensable necessity of life, then that is its point. It isn't to be followed or maintained or held onto for rewards or because it can bring you fringe benefits or dividends. It is an end in itself ... an indispensible end in itself. Sobriety is an objective upon which you can place no value anymore than you could try to place a value on your life.

After the Old Ideas, What?

The second week we asked ourselves the question, "Is it necessary to have a spiritual experience in order to maintain sobriety?" We defined spiritual experience as its set forth in the appendix to the book ALCOHOLICS ANONYMOUS as being a slow, gradual change in a person's attitude towards reality. It is not the sweeping, religious experience or supernatural happening that many think is necessary, but what is set forth in the book that really, in the great majority of all of us, is what really took place. That, over a long period of time, with a lot of effort and a lot of work, there came a gradual change in our reaction to the world around us, to ourselves, and to the people in our world. With that kind of a definition of spiritual experience, you'll remember that technically, the answer to that question would be "no." It's not necessary to have a spiritual experience in order to achieve and maintain sobriety. You don't have to be anything. You don't have to get anything. You maintain sobriety by staying away from the first drink and in order to do that, you don't have to be virtuous, you don't have to be spiritual, you don't have to be rich, you don't have to be poor, and you don't have to be anything. There's only one thing that has to be in your mind and that is you value being sober more than you value being drunk. Based on that evaluation, you have made a choice.

However, if you extend this question and ask yourself if you want to have a life worth staying sober for, then the answer

The Rest of Your Life

is obviously, "yes." A spiritual experience would have to happen. There would be no other way to do it. That week we talked about the steps of AA; the first five steps that put this spiritual experience into motion.

The third week we asked ourselves the question, "What are the old ideas?" The old ideas that we arrived here with and that have brought us to the state where we have to seek help from a Power greater than ourselves, and from our fellow human beings. We discovered that we, as alcoholics and as neurotics, were motivated all our lives by an unholy trinity of guilt and anger and fear. That, in order to survive, and maintain some kind of torment and haunting fear, we had embarked on a double-pronged program of balancing a neurotic need for approval against an equally strong motivating factor of a need to dominate, a need to be the strongest, a need to excel, to compete, to humiliate.   Last week we asked, "If this was the trinity we served, if these were the masters that we served and if this was our desire, then how did we implement these two motivations that were really wiping each other out   all the time and causing the tension?" After all, the definition of tension is conflict. It is two opposing forces pulling in opposite directions that create tension. Then we took up what we might call "the neurotic nine"; the nine little games or little techniques that we thought we were putting together as a do-it-yourself survival kit, when, in fact, what we were doing, slowly but surely, with great

After the Old Ideas, What?

intelligence and great ability and skill was slowly destroying ourselves. I'd like to refresh your memory so we can go onto tonight's subject. I don't remember in what order I gave them, but they were: religion, booze (or any other chemical that can be taken to change your reaction to reality), sex, the critic, the martyr, the loner, resentments, the neurotic need for infallibility, and the neurotic need for a crisis. It was quite a little kit and we examined them at length and figured out how they worked and what uses we were putting them to.

Tonight let's assume that we've all stayed along this far, we've all bought all of this. The obvious question is," If I understand where I have been and what has put me there, how in the hell am I going to get out?" We learn that self-knowledge alone is not enough, but without self-knowledge you never know what you're fighting. You're fighting phantoms. And you never know where you're going and what's putting you there. But once you see this self-knowledge ... once you find it ... there finally has to come a choice. This is what's behind the line in the book that says, "Some of us have tried to hold on to our old ideas and the result was nil until we let go absolutely."[5]

Why would we hang onto ideas that were killing us? The answer is very simple. In our state of mind, operating under the motivations and the forces that were controlling us, it was clear

---

[5] Page 58, ALCOHOLICS ANONYMOUS

The Rest of Your Life

to us that this was the only way that we survived. This was the only way that we could function. This was the only way that we could get from here to there and back again. So, you don't give up convictions like these easily. You don't let go of them overnight simply because somebody like me, or anybody else, says, "You know, Bub, these things are wrong and they're driving you down into the ground. Let go of them. just walk away from them and never say anything to them again and you'll be all right." just use that wonderful expression that you've heard so many times in AA, which I tried for years to practice..."Let go and let God." I went around literally letting go, except everything kept sticking, and I kept finding it happening this way again and again and again.

You keep the neurotic nine in mind and I'll try and tell you what I found out that wraps this up. How you can take the self-same old ideas and, with the same talent, the same energy, the same zeal that you devoted to knocking yourself out, turn this whole thing around and instead of destroying yourself, start building yourself up. I hope that it's as clear to all of you as it finally became clear to me, (if you got it in five weeks, I congratulate you) that the one thing that brought us all through the doors of an AA meeting was the conviction that of ourselves we had no worth. This was in all our minds no matter how we acted. No matter whether we were timid or grandiose, whether we were shy or belligerent, whether we wept or snarled ... this was really

After the Old Ideas, What?

what was inside of us, that of ourselves we had no worth. We were filled with self-recrimination, self-abnegation, and the great colossal self-put-down. This sometimes showed through, but most of the time we kept it hidden.

What then becomes our objective? It's to turn this around. To turn this around and not only quit not liking ourselves, but end up literally having a love affair with ourselves. I thought that this would be pretty hard to do. I remember one time after about six months with the meter running; I said to my doctor, "Doctor, what are we doing? What are we after? What is our goal, Doctor?" And he said, "Mr. McGinnis, it's very simple. We're trying to improve your self-esteem." Little did I know then that I was going to become one of his most successful patients.

Let's try to go through some of these things. There are seven. It's a very lucky number and some of you have heard them before. I'm repeating them tonight for two reasons. Number one, they become more valid in my life with each passing day, and number two, so many of you have asked me to repeat them, I don't see any point in trying to come up with new ones to entertain you when these work. At least as far as I'm concerned, they work. I'm going to give them to you in the order I think they have to be worked although nothing ever falls into any perfect order.

Now you're going to run into your number one stumbling block ... the number one thing that is going to be the first

The Rest of Your Life

rule because it's what you arrived here with. It's what kept you going for years on the darkest day and through the longest night. This was really what kept you in there plugging away and you're going to hang onto it. The first rule I'm going to give you is: *Renounce the Remorse.*

I remember some years ago reading in the works of a theologian (who shall remain nameless) this line," Shame is the next best thing to virtue." And I believed it. I thought, well, that's good. I'm glad I read that and I'm glad that he promulgates this theory because I've got so much of this shame that I must be the next best thing around that you can find. I hesitate to think how much harm this theory has done. But it is very widely held. If you can't be a saint, the next best thing to do is go around killing yourself because you're not a saint. Now, this looks like a virtue, so why should you want to let go of it? Let's pick up this remorse in our mental fingers and try to see what it's made up of. Let's see if it's this great thing that we think we should cling to and that really makes us pretty great people because we're very, very sorrowful that we've been so rotten and made all these mistakes.

What is this remorse? What is this regret? When we really look at it, It is nothing more or less than more of the anger that is turned in upon yourself It is a sense of outrage that you have failed, that you haven't been the perfect person that you thought you ought to be and that you were told you should be and that was

After the Old Ideas, What?

constantly held out for you to be. How many times have you heard yourself saying, "How could I do that? How could I think that? How could I be that way? What the hell's the matter with me?" It goes back to that childish thing that we talked about when we were very little, and the figures of authority in our childhood ... the giants that shaped and molded us kept saying, "You've got to be better. Do it better, do it better, and do it better. You can be better if you just try. You can be better if you just try." So it's this same thing turned in on us again. The remorse, the regret, the sense of outrage that we have failed.

Remorse and regret are really nothing, more or less, than pride turned in against us. When you look at it this way then you see it for the neurotic thing that it is and you realize that it is a further handicap, and you see the trouble with this kind of thing. After you've thought it all over and you realize and feel how terrible you have been and you feel so sorry about it and you're so filled with remorse and regret, what is the logical thing to do? The logical thing to do is to go out and celebrate this by being more guilty. Do some more things that you can feel more remorseful for and this way, we keep it going. We never get around to changing. We don't have to ... we can just go along feeling sorry. Besides, this keeps giving all of our friends and all of our family and all of our relatives this wonderful out, that he would be such a wonderful

The Rest of Your Life

man if he could only find out what's wrong. So, the number one rule is: *Renounce the Remorse*.

This leads right into the second one that I call *Look at the Evidence*. I'm going to try to give you examples out of my own life of what I mean by these because that's the only way that I know. Maybe they will not apply to you but you can adapt them to whatever it means from your point of view. These old ideas seem so logical and the reason we cling to them is because they do seem so right. Many of them we were taught, and what makes it doubly difficult is nearly all of them are partially true.

For instance, this is where I learned that I had to look at the evidence. I arrived in AA with the conviction that I, being a cradle member of the one true, universal church, had, at my fingertips, all that I needed to know. I knew how to face life. I knew how to cope with it and I knew how to do everything. Now, if that couldn't work, then what else was going to be found? It was obvious there couldn't be anything else, so I would dismiss it. I finally had to look at the evidence. What was the evidence? The evidence was that, whatever was the matter, it wasn't working. That was the evidence. Either I was wrong, or the religion was wrong, or the way I was using it was wrong. I don't want to carry this forward to where all of a sudden people will interpret it that I'm giving a blanket condemnation to religion. I don't mean that at all. I mean that what I had to back up and see was that the evidence

After the Old Ideas, What?

showed that something was wrong. Something that I was doing was seriously wrong or I would be getting better results. This was the thing I found that I had to learn to do. I had to be willing to do this. I had to have enough of an open mind, enough that would bring me, by sheer logic, to examine everything in my life. I did it with my job. After a period of time of putting forth my best efforts and constantly having what could be called less than perfect results, I had to look at it and say, "Are all these fine rules that I formulated for myself, (and I had a S.O.P. for my department, a standard operating procedure, that single-spaced was about this thick, and by God, they followed it), not bringing very good results"? This was a place where I had to look at the evidence. And I ask, urge, and suggest that you do the same. Whatever area in your life where you feel that ... this is it ... this is right ... there can't be any flaw in this ... I've gone all through this and I've arrived at this and this is the way it is ... if the results that those convictions are producing are not constructive, then I think that, somewhere along the line, you have to back up and look at the evidence.

Number three is a game that I find I have to play constantly called *Who's Who*. You'll remember, if you were here for the third session, that we talked about the guilt and anger and fear that started as a child ... as a very tiny child. And, in our childish way, we came up with a neurotic way to cope with it. All

The Rest of Your Life

of us had certain figures of authority in common. They were the mother, the father, the teachers, the relatives, the older brother or sister. There were all these people who shaped and molded what we became. Where we first learned to "cope" was in this childhood environment.

The main thing that the neurotic does ... the thing that he does all along until he finds out that he's doing it ... is to keep reacting to the present as if it were happening to him in the past. In other words, everything that comes into his life he relates back to how he learned to cope with it as a child. So, he turns the major influential important figures of the present into corresponding figures from the past. Bosses become fathers. Wives become mothers. Husbands become fathers, or sons, or rivals. We set up a drama and we keep dealing with these people, not in the role that they really are, but in what we found, as a child, we could cope with, or thought we could cope with. I tried to turn every boss I ever had, whether they were younger or older, dumber or smarter, into my father. I never ever really was intent on anything except making the boss like me (Because, you see, if he liked me best like I tried to get Dad to like me), then he would take care of me, he would protect me, he would see that things would be all right. I remember how I use to read about paternalistic government and think, "Oh, isn't that awful! That's bad. We should all be rugged individuals and every man for himself." And here I was, you know,

After the Old Ideas, What?

just seeking fathers everywhere. Every time one showed up, if he had on a pair of pants and looked halfway intelligent, there was a candidate.

I did this in other ways too, and I'm sure that you have. When you find yourself playing this game ... when you find yourself sometimes treating those who are important to you in certain ways and there is a certain undesirable result coming from it ... sit down and think about it. Think ... do I look upon her as my wife or do I look upon her as my mother? What am I trying to get her to be? In any close situation, what really makes the difference between whether you're going to function or whether you're not? I don't mean that every time you walk out onto the street and get on a bus that you have to say to yourself, "Who the hell is this?" No. Or, if you walk into the elevator and you don't know them, and you feel a little funny thing going on, that you have to say, "I wonder who I've turned that person into"? It's the people who are in your very intimate circle. The people, who make the difference; the bosses, the children, the husbands, the wives, the lovers, the mistresses, etcetera, etcetera, etcetera. They all have roles. There's many a wife who's a daughter and many a mistress who's a mother, or vice versa. Some of them are even sisters.

Let's move on to one of the things that I have to keep relearning over and over again. The fact is that I have to keep relearning all of these things. That's what makes it interesting. Try

The Rest of Your Life

to remember this one: *Effort is Everything*. From here on in, I urge you to consider dropping from your vocabulary, for all time, phrases like ... best of my ability, all or nothing at all, ...and all that ilk that have their roots in this tyrannical need for perfection. Remember that one of the neurotic nine was the need for infallibility. Another name for it is the perfectionist complex. I think probably there isn't any more serious stumbling block to recovery from serious neurotic tendencies than this insistence, this demand that everything in your life must be perfect. You demand perfection of other people, you demand it of institutions, but above all, you demand it of yourself and this is founded in guilt. This awful feeling of unworthiness that we, of ourselves, have no worth therefore we don't dare be wrong. We don't dare be less than perfect. We have got to get it right.

Yesterday morning I spent two hours with the priest that I took my fifth step with some fifteen years ago. I hadn't seen him in a while. He's now the Prefect of St. John's Seminary at Camarillo. I drove up and he and I spent two hours in his office and another half hour walking through the grounds. When we got all finished, he and I were in complete agreement that still, in me, the biggest thing I have to constantly concern myself with is this stubborn, subtle, omnipresent struggle for perfection. This inability to accept myself as a fallible human being that works in me constantly, over and over and over again.

After the Old Ideas, What?

I was telling him how, a long time ago, I was reading the New Testament and I came across the place where somebody asked Christ, the Master, what he must do? And Christ turned to him and said, very simply, "Take up your cross and follow me." And I said, "Am I right, Father, in the assumption that I made then, that the cross that Christ was referring to is the cross of our human nature?" He said "yes," as every theologian from the very beginning has agreed, this is what He's referring to. He wasn't referring to some kind of great burden, some kind of special thing He was going to give you. It was the cross of the day in and day out fallible human nature that you were to live with. And, in learning to live with it, be ten times more at peace with the weakness within you than you are in this constant striving for perfection.

Long after the theologians promulgated it, all the psychiatrists and psychologists agreed that every man's weaknesses are also his greatest strengths, and vice-versa. His greatest strengths become his greatest weaknesses. That's the way they work. So, you cannot despise these weaknesses and you cannot try to overcome them. Turn them around and properly regard them and they become your greatest strengths. Knowledge of your fallibility, an acceptance of it ... an unqualified acceptance of it ... becomes the greatest strength and the greatest safeguard and the greatest force for stability in your life.

The Rest of Your Life

The next one I call ... *Break the Circle*. The last time I tried to tell this to somebody and discuss it with them, I finally saw that I was getting it to them all wrong ... or else they were hearing it wrong ... because what they got in their head was that, for the rest of their life, they were going to have to stand, like a dumb ox, while the human race rained blows upon their head. I wouldn't do that for Nobody! And I don't advise you to do it. Here again, this applies to those situations in your life that really matter. If you only see someone about once every two years, you don't have to worry about breaking the circle ... it's broken. It's the day in and day out, the close family, the job. This is where you live your life and where you have to apply this daily. This game is so common. I've yet to find the life situation of a person where it doesn't exist. The only thing I can call it is the Dance of Death that two people get into. They get locked in this dance and when one moves forward, the other moves forward. When one moves back, the other moves back. It is a dance and they have to do it. They have to cooperate. They don't look like they're cooperating but they are and that's the funny part. This is what took me so long to see. I'll illustrate it with a situation out of my own life.

This situation certainly got to me. It nearly drove me up the wall. In fact, it did drive me up the wall. In this kind of situation, the roles are always unconsciously understood. Each one knows his own role and he plays it or else they don't have a dance.

After the Old Ideas, What?

Somebody leads and somebody follows. There is a signal that is given when the dance is to begin and they go into it. I had a dance of death with my boss for nine years. We learned the steps real good. My role was the role of the Humiliate. He had the role of the Humiliator. Now we had to react or we didn't have a dance, and I'll tell you how it was done. I'm sure that you can now figure out where it goes on in your life. Generally, these dances are done with audiences ... children, co-workers, neighbors, good friends. It's much better when these dances are performed with an audience because each one can get his role in there. This is the way it happened with me.

Generally there was a conference. It could happen at any hour of the day or night but when we really did the dance at depth ... when the symphony orchestra played, back in the wings, was generally when there was a conference. There was some kind of a big, important decision that had to be made and the Humiliator, my boss, sat there. We all trotted out our little wares and then it would be my turn. The signal would be given.

"Well, let's see what Mac has." That was the signal ... the dance was going to begin. Right away I thought "Yes, yes, strike up the music." Then I trotted out my wares ... always on the defensive... pushing, pushing, pushing. This is the greatest; this is the finest; I've given this a lot of thought; I've prayed over it, you know, and here it is and it's great, and it's the only thing that can solve the problem.

"What in hell made you think that would work?" My turn ... and we go into frothing at the mouth ... denunciations, accusations of being misunderstood, and accusations of not knowing what the situation was with the client, etcetera, and etcetera. It always ended up the same. I always played right into his hand. The dance always had the same conclusion because I always ended up with the fraternal father who patted the son on the head and said, "You know, Mac, you're so emotional. You just can't take any kind of objective criticism. It's true you have a certain amount of talent, but goddammit, Mac, you're going to have to learn to be an adult." And then I would go away defeated. I had played my little role and he had played his and the dance had been danced. It never failed. We did this over and over and over again.

Finally, I saw my role and saw that the only way this circle was going to be broken was that I would have to change my role. Now, how do you change your role? He's the boss. Am I going to be able to become the Humiliator? No, not and stay around for a while. The only thing I could do was quit being the Humiliatee and that's what I call *Breaking the Circle*.

There came a day and I don't know how it ever happened. I thought about it a lot. I was doing a lot of work on it ...

After the Old Ideas, What?

spending a lot of money on it ... doing a lot of praying, etc. One day the signal was given. "Let's see what Mac has." The same old signal and this time, Mac, who had also decided to put into effect the next rule we're going to take up, laid his stuff out very matter of factly, as though he were in front of a bunch of people he'd never seen before. Now, this takes a little bit of acting and it takes a little bit of control and little things are going on in your stomach and you might break out in a sweat ... but it can be done.

Now came step number two in the dance. "What in hell made you think that would work? I never saw anything like that in my life. What do you think of it, guys?"... Mumble, mumble, and mumble. Time for my step, and I said, "You know you may be right. You know the account a lot better than I do. After all, you're the regional manager. You were once the account supervisor on this account and I'm sure that you probably have a better judgment of this than the client himself. So, I think you ought to make the decision whether or not it should be shown." And I left. I wasn't humiliated. He had his dance right back in his lap because he had to make the decision now. I had broken the circle. I had to do it again and again and again, but you know what happened? If nobody dances with you when you get up to dance, you finally quit dancing. He finally got to where he quit getting up and he quit giving the signal and he found somebody else to take my place. They were all ready and willing and able to move in.

The Rest of Your Life

The name I've given to the next one is: *Let the Tailgaters Pass*. The reason I've given it that name is that I'm sure that every alcoholic has been on the road when suddenly he becomes aware, in the mirror, that there's somebody right on his tail light. Let's face it, what is your first reaction? You know damn well. Both of you rush pell-mell toward destruction because he isn't going to get past you. This goes back to that childhood thing of, be better, be better, and be better. Don't bring home just B's and Cs. Bring home all A +'s. Don't let anybody get ahead. The need to compete ... the need to dominate.

How can you take this self-same thing and turn it around? You are going to think I'm cracked because I'm going against everything that we've ever been taught. I'm going against the precepts of our culture ... the precepts of the great American dream. And I am telling you to consider this and consider it hard. I am urging you to stop competing. *Let the tailgater pass.*

You're going to say, "McGinnis, are you really standing up there, supposedly in possession of your senses, and telling me not to compete in today's world? In today's society?" That is exactly what I'm telling you to do. Because competing is the neurotic part of the activity. I'm not telling you to downgrade yourself. I'm not telling you not to employ your talents to the fullest. I'm not telling you not to give everything that comes up in your workday job, or in any area of your life, everything that you

After the Old Ideas, What?

have to give it. I'm telling you to stop making it a do-or-die competition.

I put this to the test. I put my money, and I mean that literally, I put my job where my mouth is. I put it to the test in one of the most competitive businesses around. I think that, next to show business, advertising is just about as cutthroat as anything I know of. As a matter of fact, they've discarded knives in the back. They use laser beams now. But I put it to the test. I stopped competing. I stopped this knife in the back thing. I stopped this constant put-down and I'll tell you how it worked out.

Sooner or later, your work is going to be judged by somebody who is not in the neurotic rat race with you. And no matter how much bugle-blowing the other guy has done, no matter how many knives he's thrown, no matter how much he's put you down, no matter how much he's cut your throat, sooner or later the product you've turned out or whatever you're doing is going to be evaluated by somebody who's not in that particular neurotic rat-race. He may be in another one, but he's not in that one. And he'll be able to evaluate it and I tell you that good work, talent, ability, efficiency, is so rare in this world, that you don't need to worry about how good you are at cutting the other fella down, if you are good at what you do.

The old saying about the path to the better mousetrap still holds true. The funny part of this is that you do better work. I

The Rest of Your Life

found that I did. When you stop wasting all the energy, all the thought, all the time, all the hatred, and give up the resentments and the staying up nights figuring out how you can get ahead of the bastard ... when you don't have to do that and can turn your energies and your talents around to the situation, to the question, to the problem ... you do far, far better work and it's much more quickly recognized. In any area of your life where you're in competition, stop competing. *Let the tailgater pass*. Let him run on ... to his doom. You'll get there in time to see the ambulance taking him away.

The last one is: *Is the Price Right?* This one you don't play very often but, boy oh boy, when the time comes, you really have to play it. Everything in life has a price tag. Success has a price tag. Failure has a price tag. If you're going to stay sober, that has a price tag. If you're going to go down on skid row and drink for the rest of your life that has a price tag. Virtue has a price tag. Sin has a price tag. Everything has a little price tag on it and you have to pay it ... you have to pay it. Somewhere along the line, in your life, in situations that really matter to you, you have to sit down and say, "Can I afford to pay the price for that? Do I want it? Do I want what it offers bad enough to pay the price tag that's on it?" And then you're able to make a choice.

For instance, let's go back to the situation that bugged me for so many years. I don't know how many times in the nine

After the Old Ideas, What?

years that this situation with my boss existed, that I seriously considered leaving the agency, resigning and going and finding another job. There were advantages in both alternatives. If I got out of this situation, there was the advantage of being out of it. The drawback was that I had a great equity in this agency; I had been with them for years. I was a stockholder. I had profit sharing and I had a severance agreement with them. I was a vice-president so I had recognition with this company and no matter where you go in the agency business, no matter what kind of title you have hanging on you, or what kind of proof you take with you, you have to prove yourself.

I had to sit down and make a choice. I had to pay a price and this is where you weigh. You weigh what you want, knowing that there is a price tag on it and that you are going to have to be willing to pay it. Believe me, I think that the best definition of emotional maturity is the ability to choose what you want to do ... to make a choice as to what course of action you wish to follow ... and then accept the consequences that go with the choice. The two can't be separated. You can't make the choice and then refuse to pay the price tag. That's emotional immaturity. The two have to go together. That's the name of the game. To have the ability to live your life by saying "I choose this course of action. I have weighed it. I know what the price tag is and now I am willing to pay whatever the tariff asks." And once you've done that, then

The Rest of Your Life

keep your mouth shut. You just make a bargain with yourself and you keep your mouth shut. You don't go through life every time you can get anybody in a corner and start crying about trying to have your cake and eat it too.

If you play this game, you don't have to get on the phone so often, or run around doing so much advice asking like, "What do you think I should do?" Because, of course, what you're trying to do in that situation is to get somebody to agree with the course of action you have already decided to take and assure you that there isn't going to be any price at all. And since somebody's always going to think the way you do at any given moment, and somebody else is going to think the other way, one day you have to make up your own mind anyway. You might as well decide that you're going to be happy on your own time or be unhappy on your own time. There's no use getting anybody else into the act because they don't have to pay the price. They can give you all kinds of advice, but you're the only one who can choose ... you're the only one who can pay the price. I'd like to end here because I want to save a little time for some questions but I'll give you a little secret. It's something very simple and it took me a long, long time to discover it. If you want to take a giant step tonight toward peace of mind and hold onto it for the rest of your life, drop two words out of your thinking and out of your vocabulary. Never let them come past your lips again as long as you live. They will come into your

After the Old Ideas, What?

head, but you'll never let them be spoken again. The two words are: *If only*. This is the litany of the defeated. This is the refrain of regret. All it does is keep pulling the rug out from under you. These words will come into your mind because it's part of the remorse, part of this neurotic need to punish, part of this neurotic need to regret, part of this neurotic need to put yourself down ... to compare yourself with others, to be constantly finding fault with yourself as you were found fault with as a child. This is a game that you are playing that is destroying you. It can negate everything that I've told you or suggested for you to think about. It can negate everything that you're trying to do.

When that phrase comes into your mind, I'll tell you four words to put in its place. When you find yourself, on some day, thinking ... If only, if only, if only...try putting these four words in their place ... *There is always now. There is always now.* That's what there always was, and that is what there will always be. Always, always, always in those years that are past, there was always now. And when you are one minute away from your last breath, there will always be now.

The Rest of Your Life

Question and Answer Period

How do you renounce the remorse?

I thought that the whole thing we did in picking it up in our mental fingers took care of that. We realized that it is an anger directed against ourselves. A disappointment in ourselves that is an echo of that same childhood thing of constantly being found fault with. Constantly being told that we could do better. You simply don't do it anymore ... you don't do it. And you are capable of that. See, this *if only*, and the remorse are all tied together. In the first place, you can't do anything about the past. It's gone. It's dead. The only thing you can do with the past is learn from it, that's the only use it has for you. Any other use you make of it is going to be a neurotic and a destructive use. You quit regretting it, you quit being remorseful about it. You just stop, that's all. Just like you stopped drinking. Just like you stop anything else, you just don't do it.

After the Old Ideas, What?

There's no special trick. You realize what it is, that it is a neurotic thing. That it is not a virtue and it does not make you good in the eyes of God to go around saying "Gee whiz, why did I do that? I'm sorry, I'm sorry, I'm sorry." This does not make you into a saint, and if it doesn't make you into a saint ... what's the use? Let it go.

How do you stop competing without falling by the wayside?

That's what I tried to bring out. I was in a highly competitive business and I stopped competing. I don't mean that you come to work and sit there with your hands folded until they fire you. I mean you do what you have to do. You do the duties that are given to you with everything that you've got. But you don't add to these all kinds of little hanky panky ... like tearing the other guy down, trying to outsmart him, trying to put yourself up at the other guy's expense. You see, anytime you show yourself off to a good advantage, it won't work unless you show somebody else off to a disadvantage. And this is all I'm saying ... you simply stop, whether the business is competitive or not. Let's take a bricklayer. I don't know anything about bricklaying and maybe it's a highly competitive business, but it finally comes down to the guy who lays the brick best and the bricks stay where they're put. He keeps getting work, I'm sure.

The Rest of Your Life

In thinking about myself and trying to apply these rules of self knowledge, there's a tendency for the real world to become unreal and it's like watching a movie of the real world while I think about myself ... What should I do?

I never had this. I was able to think about myself while juggling, so I really don't know. I can't imagine, if you're having a conversation with somebody in your job that you can have a blank look come across your face and you start thinking about yourself. But I believe that you can wash your teeth, shave, and a lot of other things ... drive cars, sit alone ... I've been able to think about myself while carrying on a conversation. As a matter of fact, I was having a lot better conversation with myself while I was carrying on the other conversation. I'm sorry; I don't know how to answer that question. If the real world starts getting unreal, I'd quit doing what you're doing. If you're on the freeway and it begins to look unreal, go back to doing what you used to do.

One of the members says that maybe what you are talking about is self-involvement. I do not know any technique by which you can find out what is going on inside of you and what is motivating you and what is causing you to think and feel the way you think and feel without becoming involved with yourself. I don't know of any other way that you can do this. Now I know that it is a great maxim to say get interested in others. I'm going back

After the Old Ideas, What?

again to the book where it says ... see to it that your own house is in order ... because obviously you cannot transmit something you do not have. And mind you, I am not putting down working with others because, if self esteem does not express itself and find an outlet in sharing your own feeling of self-approval with everyone in your life, then you don't really have self-approval. I think that it goes back to the precept in the Bible...Love your neighbor as you love yourself. I don't see how in the world you can live your life without being, at all times, involved with yourself. I think that probably we are talking here in a semantic tightrope feather-dance of whether you are involved with yourself or not. If working with others so you don't think about yourself becomes a substitute for what I've been talking about, in my own actual experience of trying to do just that for three and a half years, it didn't work. All it did was postpone and make more difficult and more agonized and more tormenting what I finally had to do. I can only speak for myself. As I say, if anything is causing you distress, then let's go back to rule number two...Let's look at the evidence. Whatever you're doing, if the results are not good, then back up and look at the evidence and arrive at your own decision.

In the beginning when I tried to think about myself, it was too painful and it got mixed up. Now after a certain amount of sobriety, I'm starting again, and it's easier.

The Rest of Your Life

I forgot to point this out tonight. If you're new and you've only been sober a matter of days or weeks, you have only one thing to do. You stay away from the first drink. Do anything else. This stuff that I'm talking about will come when you feel that you have to do it. And, as a matter of fact, when you feel that you have to do it that is the only time that it will ever be of use. Maybe you will never feel the need for it.

These are not Ten Commandments that I've been talking about. They are things that I had to do and I've been putting them out in front of you only with the idea that they may be of help to you. I know that a lot of times, when I, or anybody else, but probably me in these last few weeks, stands up here putting up all this stuff, that probably and very legitimately, some of you have thought, "I wonder if that joker ever puts his money where his mouth is?" I've tried to tell you tonight some instances where I have done the things I have told you, I have lived. These aren't theories that I have read and brought here out of a book. And I want to close with one instance that happened just recently.

Last October, when I was seriously considering whether or not I should resign, I called a friend of mine in New York. He's in our New York office and a member of the board of directors and he's been one of the closest friends that I've had in the company. I told him how I felt ... that I wanted to go away, that

After the Old Ideas, What?

I figured that I'd put up with this long enough. Now, mind you, I was leaving this agency about ten or twelve years be- fore I needed to. His advice to me was, "Well, Mac, why don't you, just sit there and let the meter run." I put the phone down and I thought, "Thank God I called him because he's a great, wise, practical guy and that's exactly what I'm going to do. I'm going to sit here. I'm going to take it easy and I'm going to enjoy myself and I'm going to let the meter run. I'm going to let all that stock and profit-sharing and all that stuff pile up and ten or twelve years from now I can walk out of here and I'll really be healed." About an hour later, this thought kept going on in my mind and, all of a sudden, it dawned on me that it was *my* meter that was running. It was my meter that was running, and ladies and gentlemen, the day you were born, the flag went down and the meter has been running ever since. If I could leave you with one thought, it's ... *making the trip count*...because you're paying for it whether you like it or not. The flag is down.

When you wake up in the morning, it will be the beginning of the first day of the rest of your life and I tell you ... *make it count...make it count*. Be unreal. Make mistakes. There's too much fear being preached in AA today, in my opinion. You hear it from all sides. The newcomer comes in and he's given a list of don'ts that would stagger a mule. Don't get married...don't not get married. Don't change your job ... don't not change your job.

The Rest of Your Life

Don't eat ... don't not eat ... don't diet ... don't not diet ... don't stand up ... don't sit down ... don't go there ... don't go here. I'm going to tell you ... DO!

There are only three "don'ts" that I'd tell you. *Don't pretend. Don't be afraid. Don't run away*. I don't care how young you are or how old you are ... it is later than you know. So make it count. *Life is for the living ... dares to live*! Dare to move out, dare to be vulnerable, dare to be hurt. Dare to experience life. You've been running away all your life. And if you have found something in AA that works for you, don't hold onto it and clutch it. Don't turn this organization, I beg of you, into a ghetto where we're going to hide and lick our wounds, coining childish little defensive words like normsie, and alkie, while we point to "out there" and God, oh God ... and we all hang together in here in fear, and hold each other's hands. If you've found something in here ... compassion and understanding and dignity, take it in your hands and go out there ... out there and live it. Experience life to the fullest. It's the only one you'll ever have.

I want to thank you for the privilege of being with you these past five weeks. If I have helped you in any way, I hope that you will reward me by saying a little prayer for me. If I haven't helped you, you are going to have to pray for me...so I win either way. In a few weeks I'll be setting my feet on the land of my

After the Old Ideas, What?

ancestors for the first time in my days. That's how I'm trying to make the rest of my life count.

I want to leave you with an old Irish wish. May we all, all of us, be a half hour in heaven before the devil even knows we're dead. Thank you.

The Rest of Your Life

Sharing

San Mateo
Three Years Later

The Rest of Your Life

Sharing

Introduction

The first five chapters are from a series of seminars McGinnis gave in 1968. This is from a talk he gave in 1971, one of the last times he shared. It has been transcribed and reprinted here. It is possible to learn from him how life can happen to us sober when we are challenged to put into practice what we have heard and learned through the years. It isn't always easy, but it is possible if the foundation is solid. Shortly after this talk, and perhaps providing some explanation of how our physical condition can affect our reaction to life situations, Allen was diagnosed with cancer. He died of that cancer in November of 1972, sober and still giving hope and encouragement to those who were there.

The Rest of Your Life

Sharing

Sharing

GOOD EVENING, ladies and gentlemen. My name is Allen Reid Francis Xavier McG. And, I am an alcoholic.

Anything I say here can be held against me, but not against AA. There are only two groups in AA that I like to stress that to ... newcomers, and old timers. And if we all remember it, then nothing I say here, or any other speaker from any other AA podium anytime and anywhere, need ever distress you, or bug you. As a matter of fact, there's always a great possibility that something that is said might help you, as well as the one who says it. Please, God that will be the way it is tonight.

I'm always a little irritated and disenchanted with speakers from AA podiums who begin by telling you how nervous they are. It always sounds like special pleading to me, kind of saying ... "look, I'm shy and I'm sensitive and I'm fragile ... so, cooperate!" Well, I'm nervous tonight. Damn nervous. But it isn't

The Rest of Your Life

at all because I'm shy or sensitive or fragile. I wouldn't be here if I was shy and sensitive and fragile ... I'm about as shy as a bull.

Why I am nervous is a thought that keeps ... it's a question, really ... that keeps recurring in my mind over the years. I think it probably first hit my brain when I was about a week old and on my way to St. Joseph's Church in Crebs, Oklahoma, to be baptized, and the question is, "I wonder what kind of an impression I'll make?" And, that is why I am nervous.

I have a problem in that I have now been sober longer than I drank. And, as the years go by, and I'm asked to speak at AA meetings, I quickly review these 19 years in my mind, and I think ... well, dear God, what will I talk about? Obviously, when you have been sober for 19 years, more than 19 years, you can pile up an awful lot of experience ... that important thing that we're supposed to share. The magnificent thing about this experience that we pile up in AA is that we remember it. And, because we remember it, we learn from it; and because we have learned from it, there is the natural wish to want to pass it on to those who are following us. As a matter of fact, that is really, in my opinion, what the AA Fellowship is all about. And, since, of course, this has happened to me, and I have lived this experience and learned from it, it is of intense importance to me and I don't see how I can leave out one tiny little word of it. But, in case you think that you're

Sharing

going to be subjected to 19 years ... take heart. I'm simply just not strong enough to stand up here that long.

I'll try tonight to telescope it...how it all finally came together and what brings me to this moment here tonight. It's not going to be easy to do, but I'll try. It's never easy to be rigorously honest about yourself. It's so pleasant to be rigorously honest about everything else, but about yourself, it's a little tough. Since I have been sober now longer than I drank, thank God I can spare you from any drunk-alog. As a matter of fact, my drinking was just exactly like your drinking. The longer I'm in AA, the more distressed I am that nobody comes up with any new thing, really. We all drank too much, too fast, too long. As a matter of fact, my drinking can find a parallel in the old story about the bobcat who mistakenly courted the skunk and was later heard to remark, "Well, I enjoyed as much of it as I could stand." And, in one sentence, that takes care of my 19 years of drinking. I stayed in there as long as I could, and I didn't surrender easily.

I don't think anybody ever approached this fellowship with more of a closed mind than I did. As a matter of fact, I got here while headed in exactly the opposite direction. It was my intention to take what was left of my substance and go down to Skid Row and there, among my people, end my days anonymously ... a misunderstood genius to the very last. I don't dare get off on telling you how I got to AA because it is a fascinating story. I regale people with it for hours. And, if I dare start, we just won't get there.

Due to an unholy alliance that developed between my boss, my pastor, my physician, the one friend I had left, and two Irish conspirators from AA, instead of finding myself in the anonymity of Skid Row, I found myself in the somewhat belligerent anonymity of Alcoholics Anonymous ... an environment to which I took an instant and violent dislike ... among people I decided were definitely not my people. But I was trapped, totally and completely trapped.

When anyone who has anything at all to do with you, including one of God's direct representatives, has decided that for you a sojourn in a land called AA is highly to be desired, then anyone who was feeling as weak and weary and guilty as I was is not likely to give any visible signs of rebellion. So I went to AA after this 12th Step call that was paid on me by these two Irish 12th Steppers. It was a very spiritual 12th Step call. They came into the apartment, took one look at me and said, "Do you have any money?" And I said, "Well, (chuckle) wouldn't you know, yes, I have money, why do you ask?" They said, "To our practiced eye, you're about five minutes away from the DT's and we think you should be placed in a sanitarium." And I said, "Can I choose the sanitarium? At some of them I have credit." They said, "Yes, you can choose the sanitarium." So I asked to be taken to one that had

Sharing

come to be my favorite. I had found it after much research. It was located on Fairfax Avenue in West Hollywood, just two blocks away from my parish church. I figured that if I worked everything all right and God was kind, I would be in Dr. M's sanitarium and he would come in with a shot of paraldehyde while Father O'Toole came in with the last rites, and it would all come out even.

It was from this spiritual background that I approached my first AA meeting. I have heard many speakers on AA podiums since, say that it was all those happy people at their first AA meeting that won them over. Well, this was a large meeting. It was on a Saturday night on Hollywood Boulevard, in the basement of the Garden Court Apartments, just opposite the Cinegrill in the Hollywood Roosevelt. That is a watering hole that you Northerners would not know anything about, I think. But besides alcohol, you found other divertissements there. As I walked down the stairs of this basement entrance, I remember looking across Hollywood Blvd. at the Cinegrill thinking ... well, goodbye. It's all over. I'm going off to this place where everybody thinks I ought to be, and it will be just my luck for it to work. I may become healthy, probably a little sane, maybe even a little rich ... but, I will be dead ... because I am going to be sober the rest of my natural life and I couldn't contemplate it.

However, as I said, there wasn't any way I could get out of it. I looked at those happy people, I listened to them, and I

The Rest of Your Life

wanted to go outside and vomit. I said to myself, if they're really this happy, they are morons. They simply don't know that I and the world are coming unglued. And they're sitting in here laughing and using little code words on each other. I knew they were code words because they lifted their eyebrows when they talked to each other. One would come up to the other one and say, "Hi, first things first." And the other one would say, "Yep, and easy does it." Then they would part, having exchanged worlds of information.

I also was sure that they were all stockholders in foreign coffee plantations. I knew of no other reason that could explain why they drank gallons of this beverage that they called coffee. Now, over the years, I have looked at this habit that we have. I've seen newcomers come in shaking, sweating, not knowing whether to run to the toilet or sit down, and we say, "Have a cup of coffee." Three weeks later, the poor devil, (his eyes are like saucers) says, "When will I sleep?" And we say, "Don't worry. Nobody ever died of insomnia. Have a cup of coffee." I don't think it will ever change. Talk about getting sober ... in spite of.

But I was trapped, and so I did what I always did in those days when I found myself with my back up against the wall and in a situation that was not to my liking, I adapted. And the way that I adapted was always the same ... I sincerely pretended. Looking around at my new surroundings, I knew that this

Sharing

technique was going to payoff better here than it ever had anywhere else.

It is believed that in Alcoholics Anonymous, in our humility and in our anonymity, that we have reached a milestone in this highly-to be-desired virtue, humility. But I was born and reared in a religion that is the ultimate in anonymity and in humility. You can run up the aisle to the communion rail until you wear out the carpet and no one pays the slightest bit of attention. You can run in and out of the confessional like a whirling dervish and no one bothers to notice, unless perhaps you stay a little longer than usual, and then there is some conjecture as to what new sin you may have come up with. Your virtue is known only to God and to you and this doesn't get you very much publicity. But oh, how different is the practice of the virtue of sobriety and humility in Alcoholics Anonymous. No wonder it held such fascination for me.

From the moment you hold up your reluctant hand as a newcomer, you are greeted by the moist and welcoming eyes of your neighbors. Utter strangers rush up to grab your hand and know your name and, no matter how vacantly you may stare back, you are assured over and over that you are in the right place. Your head fairly swims with the knowledge that you are everybody's life's blood. Your every word and movement is given loving attention. Even something as simple as sitting up straight in your

The Rest of Your Life

chair is taken as unmistakable evidence that you are growing. When it is discovered that you can put two sentences together without having them collide, you are asked to speak. And to a Catholic who has been living in the lifelong anonymity of the church, this is akin to suddenly being asked to say mass.

I was so delighted with the attention I was getting, that pretty soon I completely forgot how much I disliked the people who were giving it to me. I began to think to myself...I wonder how they got along for so long before I came along. And, of course, I thought they were totally, terribly brief and young. After all, those of you who may not know this, we Catholics humbly believe we are the one, the only and the true. And for someone who has been weaned on 2,000 years of St. Paul, St. Augustine, St. Thomas Aquinas, St. John of the Cross, and a few cats like that you know, something that happened 15 years ago in Akron (when I came in), between a broken down stockbroker and a defunct doctor, doesn't hold out much promise.

But I went along. It was all so simple. I read the book and I thought. .. Well, it's not very well written, but it's sound. I developed a little AA smile. You've seen it. As a matter of fact, I thought I detected it a couple of times tonight here. It's that little half-smile that says, "I'm all right; just don't get too close." And I grew. I'd been sober about two weeks when, with that acute hearing that alcoholics develop, I was at a meeting and there were

Sharing

two men about 50 feet away carrying on a conversation. I heard one of them say, "Have you noticed that new guy, McGinnis? You know he's only been sober a couple of weeks, but have you noticed how he's growing?" After that, anytime anybody looked at me, I grew ... right in front of their eyes. Fortunately, I'm a very quick study. Just about three months passed when it dawned on me that the fascination I had been exuding upon people as a newcomer had begun to fade. The people I was bumping into at meetings were not immediately healed of their disease. As a matter of fact, they started to ask me not to bump into them.

Then I made an even more shattering discovery and that was that you can sin much more efficiently sober than you can drunk. To an Irish Catholic who has depended for years upon booze to get him through sin, this can be completely and totally demoralizing. Fifteen minutes after my first meeting, I knew I was back in the be-a-better-person business and I had always failed in this business, but I thought, well, we'll try it again here. At the sanitarium where I had been and where I started my career in AA, my pastor, my boss, my priest, my doctor, my friend, and these two AA missionaries had kept coming, and every time I tried to say anything, they'd say, "Don't worry, don't worry now, you're going to AA and they know the way you've acted is not your fault. They know that you're sick and it will all be different."

The Rest of Your Life

Of course fifteen minutes after I came into AA I thought, "My God, I came in here carrying the Ten Commandments and the Six Precepts of the Church on my back and now they've given me twelve more Steps, which I need like I need a hole in the head ... but if this is what I've got to do, I'll do it. And I had made this shattering discovery that here I was, and after three months of the pursuit of sanctity; all these 12th Step calls, the meetings, the smile, the code words, the coffee, the slobbering drunks, I was the same S.O.B. that I had always been ... except I was sober and I had been robbed of my alibi because for years I had been looking up to God, priests, bosses, judges, policemen, bartenders, (I was nearly always flat on my ass, so I was nearly always looking up) saying, "Well, you know, I never would have done it if I hadn't been drunk." Now I was doing it and doing it better because I was doing it sober. I couldn't take this knowledge; I couldn't accept it because, once again, the pursuit of the virtue of sobriety had failed me. So I uttered the fateful words ... the most fateful words and notice I say fateful, not fatal ... they're fatal depending upon how you answer them ... the most fateful words an alcoholic can ever say and they are, "What is the point of sobriety if...?" What I said to myself was, "What is the point of sobriety if I don't become a better person?" And since I didn't say them out loud, no one answered me. So I resigned.

Sharing

In the two and a half months that followed, I tried committing suicide in the only way that seems to be acceptable to Catholics; I tried drinking myself to death. And I made a very useful discovery about this disease. In case you would like to know, I'll pass it on to you. You don't die fast. Instead of waking up dead, you just keep waking up day after day, week after week, just wishing you were dead. But somewhere in those two and a half months, I began to come to grips with (and I wouldn't be here tonight and there wouldn't have been the 19 years that followed if I hadn't come to grips with it) what was for me, (this first thing first), and that is ... am I really an alcoholic? And if the answer to that is yes, then do I really believe that alcoholism is truly a progressive and a fatal disease, or do I believe that it's the moral weakness that I always was taught it was and that even today in our culture, we are taught it is. Before I got to AA and after I got to AA, sobriety was a means to an end. It was something you did in order to get something else.

Before I got to AA, in the culture that shaped and molded me, drunkenness was a mortal sin. Therefore, it's absence ... sobriety ... must necessarily be a shining virtue. As a matter of fact, in the culture from which I came, it was just a notch below chastity. So when you have assumed that you are practicing the virtue of sobriety, it follows then that, since it's a virtue, you will have to be virtuous in order to achieve and maintain it. And, if

The Rest of Your Life

through very great prayer and effort you manage to achieve this shining virtue of sobriety, doesn't it also follow, as the night to day, that you should, by God, get a reward for it? You're damn right you should get a reward for it.

That's the way I came into AA, and I think that's the way everybody's been coming in behind me all these years. Until you get that straightened out in your mind, I don't think that any true recovery from alcoholism ever really begins. No matter how long you're staying sober, if you're staying sober in order to get something, or to get it back, the day will always come when what you have been staying sober to get back, you either will have not gotten it back, or now that you have gotten it, you will no longer want it. And then you will say the fateful words ... "What's the point of sobriety if I don't become a better person?" But it might very well be because even in AA, you see, we seem to talk out of both sides of our mouth at once. On the one hand we tell you that there is no moral culpability in connection with this disease at all. But then it seems in the same breath that we hasten to tell you that you're going to have to have a complete and total change of personality; you're going to have to have a spiritual awakening; you're going to have to find a Power greater than yourself; all these things in order to stay sober. AA reverberates with phrases like, "Don't do that, or...you will get drunk." So, we add fear upon fear upon fear.

Sharing

Remember I started this out, ladies and gentlemen, by telling you that anything I say can be held against me. So, while you are reacting to this, just remember it. These are my opinions, but it had to be this way with me or I wouldn't be standing here tonight.

When I came into AA 19 years ago, alcoholism had just begun to be compared to diabetes and in the 19 years that have followed, there has been a wealth of clinical evidence to establish that there is a definite correlation, a bio-chemical correlation, between these two diseases. Both of them are progressive and both of them are fatal, and both of them rest primarily on a bio-chemical change in the function of each individual. I found myself on the night of July 13, 1952, in my apartment with a half-empty can of beer, which was a beverage I loathed but it was part of my "control" drinking ... asking myself a series of questions. Now I had been drunk, suicidally drunk, for two and a half months. I had been in and out of jail. I made some jails I hadn't made before. I even made the Beverly Hills jail and that's not easy to do, and more sanitariums than I'd ever been in all the time before. On this particular night, these questions began to go through my mind. I found myself asking myself a question I asked many times before and that was, "Why is it, McGinnis, as often as you've tried to stay sober," and I will repeat that because the clue to what was wrong with my attitude towards drinking is hidden in this question, "Why

The Rest of Your Life

is it that, as often in your life as you have tried with every fiber of sincerity in your being, not just to stay sober," (do you hear that?), "not just to stay sober, but to lead the kind of life that you know you're going to have to lead if you're ever going to know a moment's peace of mind, why is it that you've always failed?"

I had asked myself that question many times before and over the years I gave myself a lot of different answers. I look back now and there was a germ of truth in all of the answers. But that night, before any of the other answers could come, a new one came in. A still, small voice that got into this drunken brain and said, "The reason, McGinnis, you have always failed is because never ever in your life have you been willing to stand still and let it hurt. You are the original no pain guy." It was the pattern of my entire life. Certainly it was the pattern of my drinking. I would stay sober until staying sober began to hurt more than I could stand it, and then I would switch. I would drink until I simply couldn't stand the pain, the sickness, the illness, the remorse, the degradation, and the humiliation any longer, and then would come the prayers and the "Oh My God's", and "I Promise You's", and I would switch back. It was the pattern of the way I practiced my religion. I was always trying to be either the St. Francis of Wilshire Boulevard or the Nero of Sunset Boulevard. It was the way I followed my job. I would do your work, my work, our work, their work, and then I would go away for two weeks and nobody could find me.

Sharing

So, I said that night, "Well, if I'm a moral coward, what in the long run would be the easiest way out?" Then I remembered two things that I had heard in this thing that I had been in for three months and which I really held in such contempt. I don't think I should say contempt because contempt would imply that I had a great deal of feeling about it, and I really didn't have a great deal of feeling about AA the first three months that I was in it. I was just going through the motions but I thought I was giving it the best shot I had and I suppose at that time I was. I remembered hearing that...it is the first drink that gets you drunk. I remembered my reaction when I heard this profound piece of wisdom. It was a reaction of rage ... that I had to come to this crazy, square, corny thing to find that out...why I couldn't have figured that out for myself! Because it was so obviously true that if I didn't take the first drink, neither God nor man could ever get me drunk.

The second thing I remembered hearing, very vaguely, was that alcoholism is a disease of a progressive and fatal nature. When I was in the sanitarium and my sponsor came to see me again and again, and I was lying on the bed doing my usual Mea Culpas, he said, "Well, for God's sakes, Allen, quit giving yourself such a bad time. After all, you have a disease." And, I thought, wouldn't you know, on this drunk, I've caught something. And that was the last thought I ever gave to a disease because, when I

The Rest of Your Life

came into AA, they started talking immediately about being a better person and that's something right away I tuned up to, because you know, I had had this neurotic need for sanctity as far back as I could remember. So that night I thought to myself, "Well, suppose I had diabetes and I'm with the same doctor that first mentioned the word alcoholic to me. Would he say to me, "Look, McGinnis, if you want to be a better person, you will stay away from the first bite of sugar?" Wouldn't he rather say, "Look, McGinnis, if you want to live, you'll stay away from the first bite of sugar and you'll take your insulin?"

There remained only one $64,000 question for me to answer then, and that was ... all right, all right, McGinnis, do you really believe it is a progressive and fatal disease? Or are you just fooling around with this? All of these ... "I will stay sober, if's" ... and with everybody else saying the same thing all around you. People looking off at horizons only they could see, and saying, "Well, for me sobriety alone is not enough." And I thought, oh that's wonderful, I like that too. I thought, do I really believe it? And then I thought, well, I'll try to look at the evidence. That night I began to play a game that I've played ever since. I call it Look at the Evidence. I thought, do I have any evidence in my own life that it is progressive? Well, you know the answer to that. I would have had to be a raving maniac to deny that it was progressive. It was so progressive it was scaring the hell out of me! Then I moved on to

Sharing

what about it's being fatal? And I thought I'd better not press that one too far. Autopsies seldom benefit the people upon whom they are performed.

So, it seemed to me the whole answer to this thing lies in do I believe I've got it and do I believe it can kill me? If the answer to that is yes, then it doesn't matter a damn whether it is a physical disease, a spiritual disease, an emotional disease, a mental disease, or a combination of all of them. The fact remains I've got to buy whether or not I think it is a killer disease. If the answer to that is yes, then comes the final question, and that is ... Would I rather live than die? And, if the answer to that is yes, then you're finally up against it. You're up against will I, can I, stay away from the first drink? Can I stay away from the first drink? I had answered this many, many times before and so have all of you. We've all stayed away from the first drink for varying lengths of time. I stayed away once for a year and-a half with no trouble at all. So I knew I could stay away from the first drink.

That night, somehow or other, it got all clear in my mind that this background that I had come into AA with, and the Catholics had no copyright on this ... God, Moslems are coming in with the same thing that, if you stay sober you should get something for it ... and that was, *if* it's a disease, then let's take all of this other stuff away from it. That night my recovery from alcoholism began because I did what I had never been able to do

The Rest of Your Life

before because I didn't know that that was what I needed to do. I separated the state of sobriety from the state of grace. And to me, in my background, they had always been completely and inextricably interdependent.

I didn't stop there. I separated the state of sobriety from the state of my soul, from the state of my health, from the state of my finances, from the state of my job, from the state of my love life, if any. I separated it from the state of everything. I simply made up my mind that I would rather live than die, and if I had a disease, I would have to stay away from the first drink, and I knew that if I took all this other stuff off of it, if I took the "be a better person" business off of it, I would be able to do it. That night I made a very simple decision and I now know it was the first authentic, 24-carat decision I had ever made in my life, because the minute I made it, I knew I'd be able to do it. A man who had wept, prayed, cried, sweated, and crawled in his efforts to stay stopped, (because I stopped ... good God ... I stopped hundreds of times, but I couldn't stay stopped), knew he would be able to do it. And that's as far as I went. I had no fear of anything else. There was no longer any more saying ... oh, my God, I promise you that I will not only stay sober, but also ... , as I had always done before and follow it up with a list that would make the Virgin Mary blanch. I was doomed before I ever got started because it had nothing to do with reality; it was done with neurotic fears.

Sharing

From that moment of July 13, 1952 ... from that night until this night...ladies and gentlemen, I have never ever had the slightest, not the slightest, desire nor need, to take a drink.

If I can quickly sketch in the 19 years that followed, you will see that I needed that foundation, *that unshakable foundation*, to know that that escape route was sealed, that bridge was burned, that door was closed, and any other metaphor or simile you wish to employ.

I didn't know where to go with this simple decision and I thought I should go somewhere with it because it was momentous to me. I couldn't see myself walking back into the vaulted cathedrals of the Roman Catholic Church saying, "Hi, I'm going to stay away from the first drink." I just didn't think this would get me much attention. So, I went back to the place where they told me the only requirement for membership was a desire to stop drinking. And I thought, this time I go back and we play the game differently. They told me that my recovery depends upon rigorous honesty; so at long last, I'm going to put them to the test. I'm going to see if they can live with rigorous honesty because I am no longer going to pretend. There will be no more half-smiles. There will be no more running up to the speaker afterwards when I've been sitting out there all the time he's up there sweating blood and talking, and I'm saying to myself ... my God, why did he ever sober up? ... And then run up afterwards and shake his hand and

The Rest of Your Life

say thank you, you helped me. Oh my God, how, in the years that have followed, I wondered how many times I've been paid back in the same coin. I thought, I'll put them to the test, I'll find out just how they are because they tell me there are no rules nor regulations, there are no sanctions, there are no directives, there is no dogma, and there is no ritual. I can't be excommunicated as long as I stay away from the first drink. We're going to find out.

There is a passage, as many of you know, in the Old Testament that says, "... The wicked are put upon the earth to exercise the just." I think for the next two years I was in AA to improve the sobriety of the members with whom I came in contact. If any of you are doubtful about this, AA will live with it. AA will stick with it. Nobody ever told me to leave a meeting. They avoided me. I would find myself sitting alone an awful lot. But nobody ever said, "Allen, you gotta go." When I had been sober about a year and-a-half, I guess that Power that's been running this for me all along decided that well, we'll do what we always have to do with this one, and we'll scare the livin' b-Jesus out of him. I found out that I was going to be transferred back to our New York office. I was going back with this advertising agency I was with. I was going back to play in the major leagues. And of course, as I had always done, then came the bargain ... "I need help, you know, I'm scared. So, why don't I get with this?" Ha!

Sharing

Right away, for the first time, I took a written inventory. I had never bothered with a written inventory because the Fourth Step meant going to confession for me and I did that like in my sleep. I went the whole bit. I did the written inventory, the Fifth Step, and I went off to New York and I discovered the first big school in AA. It's very operative back there. Its motive is right out of the book although in those days they didn't seem to have nearly as much dependence upon or respect for the Big Book as we do out here, but their motive was ... Action is the magic word. It was stenciled on their sweatshirts. It didn't matter what you were doing, just as long as you were moving.

I moved. I was the secretary of two groups concurrently. When I got off work at 5 o'clock I ran to the intergroup office and manned the phones there from 5 to 7 and then I went to a meeting. Of these groups that I was secretary of concurrently, had two meetings a week, and then, three nights a week, I rushed up to Knickerbockers Hospital where, for a time, they had an alcoholic ward and I did my Florence Nightingale number. If I could have found a candle to carry around in my hand, I would have. I remember every once in a while I would try to sit down and some worthy AA old-timer, who always assured you that his story was in the book, would say, "You're getting that look again, McGinnis, you look edgy." And I'd say, "I'm just tired." But I kept going. I think I reached the ultimate in this school, on a Christmas Eve in

The Rest of Your Life

the Manhattan State Hospital for the insane, where I MC'd a Christmas party for 450 members of that institution. They were not alcoholics; it was just something for them to come to. They were all out there, 450 of them, in various stages of catatonic withdrawal and I was up on the stage singing Jingle Bells. How many of you have gone to those lengths to get it?

Just about the time I was ready to collapse, my Higher Power moved into the scene again and I was returned to Los Angeles as the copy chief of that office in this agency. There I discovered something that seemed to have grown in my absence; the second largest school in AA activity. They have a motto too. It could be called ... Love conquers all. The main requirement for membership in this school is that you are happy. You had better damn well be happy or you are banished to that limbo reserved for those who have stopped growing. You find certain meetings ... they are known to the initiated. They were generally large meetings with wall-to wall love. They were every bit as large as this one and you had to get there early because there was a lot of kissing and handshaking that had to go on. Sometimes these meetings were so large in Southern California, that it was impossible for one member to convey his love personally to another one, so you would see them ... one sitting over here ... waving to another ... and love swept across the room. I was a faithful devotee of this school until I almost died of it.

Sharing

By this time, I'd been sober about ten years. I look back now and I'm quite sure that I was being pointed out to people as an example of what sobriety can do for you. You know ... .look at him ... see how he's prospering? See how happy he is? He's got a job, he's making money, he's got a home he's built ... he's redesigned this hill ... oh, we'll get to that later. Everything was fine, everything was fine. There was just one little thing that was wrong ... I was coming apart.

It came to a head with an obsessive hatred of my boss. I hated this man so badly that I couldn't sleep. I couldn't get him out of my mind. I don't know why I had a friend left because all I would talk about is what a bastard this man was. I did everything, everything that anybody told me. I prayed for him. I would tell you people who follow the Biblical injunction to pray for those who persecute you to be sure you want your prayers answered, because the more I prayed for this bastard, the more he prospered. God answered every prayer I ever sent up for him. He grew like the Green Bay tree while I went crazy. Finally, I made a big decision ... to do something that I really knew in my heart that I would have to give a try, although I was afraid to do it. I decided that I would go into analysis.

I went into a classical Freudian analysis that lasted four and-a-half years and in the past two years, in order to fit myself for whatever life may hold out for me in the ladder of employment, I

The Rest of Your Life

have very thoroughly engaged in and made a study of all the various other therapies that are springing up today like McDonald's hamburger stands. As you see me standing here before you tonight, I have been baptized, confirmed, analyzed, encountered, bioenergized, Gestalted, and Rolphed. So if you want to see me privately, I can tell you some astounding things. I guess all of it could be summed up in one sentence, which is more or less accurate, that all of this activity is a case of the id being examined by the odd. But for me, it worked. It changed my whole attitude, something I had never been able to do and I guess, since I believe now that God has ordered everything in my life, this must be where I had to go.

At the risk of oversimplification, since this is part of the sharing, I touch briefly on what I found out about me. I shouldn't even begin it, but I would be doing a disservice to you. I would really be mean and cruel if I brought you up to this point and then said ... you know this worked fine ... and let it go at that. I had noticed in these years of sobriety that I performed according to a pattern that I repeated over and over and over again no matter what I did. I knew somehow or other that I would have to find out what was motivating me, what was making me react, again and again and again, the way I reacted. And, at the risk of tremendous oversimplification, this is what I found out. I pass it along to you.

Sharing

It's tremendously brief and maybe I shouldn't go into it ... but enough apologies, I'll get on with it.

I found out that, as everybody else is, I was a product of my heritage, my environment and my culture that had shaped and molded every action of my life, and that mainly I had been influenced by that unholy trinity of guilt, anger, and fear, and that they had come about in that order. The guilt I am talking about is not an objective guilt, it is a subjective guilt ... a feeling of unworthiness, a personal unworthiness, that I think can best be described to you in something my mother used to always say to me when I was a child and which echoes in my brain even yet. Mom used to say to me, "Allen, be good, or God won't love you." Do you hear it? It is theologically inaccurate. My mother didn't know she was speaking heresy. She was speaking what she had been taught. "Allen, be good or God won't love you." This little tiny child now has been taught that he must perform, he must first perform, and then he wins God's love. Then he becomes worthy and from there on, all of his worth for as long as he lives will be based upon his performance.

Now, when you test this, and as I said, I can't go into it too far, it brings about naturally in the child a sense of unbearable rage and anger because he keeps failing. He keeps failing and he can't figure out why he's failing and he tries and tries and tries. But always, it's ... do it better, do it better, do it better. The unreal

The Rest of Your Life

goals that had neurotically been passed on from generation to generation-to-generation are passed on to him. So, the only thing he constantly achieves is failure. There is no such thing as good in his life. There is only better.

It took me a lifetime of pain and almost disaster to learn that in the constant pursuit of the better, to which our culture is devoted, we constantly and consistently negate the present good. So, there never is any good. It doesn't exist. There is only a better that is never attained so there is never any accomplishment...there is never any peace. Finally, out of rebellion, you begin to make this guilt objective. Since you can't express your anger any other way, you express it the only way you can and that is to finally fail deliberately. Now you have objective guilt which brings on fear. The two main fears that motivated me all my life, motivated everything that I ever did, were the fear of punishment and the fear of exposure.

I remember very clearly at quite an early age, when your world is made up of things like that, that I had divided the whole human race into two groups ... there were those who hated me, and those who didn't like me. When you are surrounded with enemies like that, you had better come up with a survival kit that will work and I came up with a survival kit that all good red-blooded, first-class, dues-paying neurotics come up with. We come up with it because it's the technique that is taught us in our culture.

Sharing

I played two games simultaneously. The first game was ... If I can make them love me, then they won't hurt me. But something tells you, since you've always failed, that you never will get everybody to love you because that's what this love has to be. Since it's going to be earned, it has to be instantaneous and universal. There must be no dissent. So, you hedge your bets by playing another game that could have as its motto ... If I am stronger than they are, and then they can't hurt me. And, of course, it never occurs to the good, blossoming, flourishing neurotic that he's constantly canceling these two things out. As a matter of fact, I remember somewhere in my analysis, I suddenly sat up from the couch and said, "I see it." The doctor said, "You see what?" I said, "I think I see what a neurotic is. A neurotic is a person who is trying simply to stand still. That's all he wants to do. He just wants to stand still. And he tries to stand still by going in exactly opposite directions at the same time." He said, "Mr. McGinnis, there have been tomes written that never described a neurotic better. May I use that?" I said, "Feel free."   We serve two tyrants. There isn't a more insatiable tyrant than the need for approval, admiration, love, recognition, status....it's a bottomless pit. There's no way to satiate this monster. As a matter of fact, I stayed awake most of last night trying to satiate it...the need ... the wondering of how I would do tonight. I made 15 different magnificent pitches last night lying awake in bed. And of course, since unfortunately

The Rest of Your Life

no one was in bed with me, they are lost to posterity. But I also used the other technique, and that is I searched for your Achilles heel. Only God knows how, in the service of this tyranny, this need for approval, how many asses we will kiss, how many people we will flatter, how many lies we will tell, how many people we will fawn upon. Generally they are people who have something that we want. Then, to hedge it, we search for their Achilles heel so that all the time we are winning them over; we are cutting them down to size. The second tyrant we serve is the need to dominate, the need to excel, the need to compete, the need to be number one ... again right out of our culture.

We live in a democracy where we say anybody can be President. Of course, today, I think it's true. But what we're really saying is everybody should be president. Maybe to some more sane people, this sounds like an activity that would be difficult to achieve. But if you're a good, red-blooded neurotic, as I am, you know it's not difficult at all. These two contradictory techniques come very naturally to you and you've developed all kinds of games to implement them. It was so simple for me, I was forever jumping up in your lap to be petted and if you didn't pet me, I jumped off your lap and I bit you. It was as simple as that. Finally I found out I had to let go of the old ideas, as it says in the book ... .let go of the techniques of this survival kit that for a long time work. It works until it begins to turn into a self-destruct kit and

Sharing

then it starts killing you. It starts killing you because it can't work indefinitely, it can't work. We have to substitute for the self-destruct games, constructive games.

I did pretty well. Everything in my life changed. My relations at the office ... I quit competing. It's hard to do, but I did it in a business that, I think next to show business, is probably the most knife-in-the-back, competitive, pressure-ridden business that you can get into, although it seems to be every business is really that way in our culture. This brings me to October of 1967. I was just back from my first trip to Europe. I had had two or three of the happiest years of my life, I think; years in which I was probably more effective, more constructive than I had ever been in my life, when I was called in and told by my management that the time had come for me to go home. I was going to be ... to use a euphemism ... retired. That's the word they use today after a certain amount of grey comes into your hair in the business I'm in, and it comes, it's coming earlier and earlier and earlier in our youth oriented culture. Somebody asked me the other day, "Allen, do you resent the young?" I said, "No, I don't resent the young at all. All I have to do is wait... their time is coming."

In this particular company that I worked for, they give you a great face-saving. I was given a going-away reception and a banquet and gifts. Also when I left I owned stock and I had a severance agreement and profit sharing. That's the other way they

The Rest of Your Life

save face and, of course, these terms are all relative. To some, the terms to describe my material gain at this point in my life, the phrase might have been ... well, he's comfortably well off. To me, from the background that I came from, I was filthy rich. I knew that my ego had been really socked because I felt, my God, my contribution, my days of contributing are over. But I've got a lot of money, it can do me the rest of my life, and so the publicity releases were made to the trades, I had meetings with the clients; they said McGinnis is going to leave to travel and write. And I left.

The year 1968 I gave myself a kind of sabbatical. I had been working, I never went to college, and I came out of school in the depths of the depression. I went to work at the age of 15 and took care of my mother and my father until I went into the Army, paying off the debts of a father who had lost all of his money and was too proud to take bankruptcy, and I'll try to tie that in very quickly to what happened.

In 1969, during the rains in California at that time, I had a series of landslides at my home. In the meantime, the retirement capital that I had ... I hate to go through all of this, but it has to be told, or else I don't end up where I should end up. I can't tell you, ladies and gentlemen, how much I should like to skip all of this. But, I would not be sharing with you if I did. I'm sorely tempted to try to do it even now. Anyway ... after being what I thought was very, very cautious and very, very sound and very,

Sharing

very practical, I put my entire retirement capital in the hands of two investment counselors and found out later on ... some months later ... that they had placed this capital. See I thought I was being smart by dividing it up between two of them ... only to find out that both of them had put me entirely in the stock market. .. in highly speculative issues and on margin.

As most of you know, all during 1969 and 1970, the bear market was with us, and while I was trying to spend thousands of dollars to get this house back in shape so I could put it on the market and sell it, the margin calls began to come. That's when I found out what margin was, and I kept trying to come up with more collateral, and finally I was being sold out in order to pay off the debts. To make a long story short, for the first time in my life, I found myself bit by bit by bit going into what I didn't know, but what I was later to find out was an acute, suicidal depression.

There may be some of you in this room who heard me last year. I'm sure there are, I know one or two, and another lady who came up and told me that she was at Bakersfield last year, on October the 25th, when 'I decided' that I would go ahead with a commitment that I had made to speak there. I don't remember much about that...mercifully God has blurred a lot of it in my mind. All I know is that I tried to do there that day what I'm trying to do here tonight, and that is to fulfill what I believe is the only

The Rest of Your Life

thing AA has ever asked of me, and that is to be rigorously honest and to share with you what is going on with me. I went ahead with the commitment that I had made. I could have, in all truth and in all honesty, said that I was too ill because I was too ill, but I decided that I would go ahead with it. All I know is, if some of you were there that day, you saw AA in action. You saw a man standing up on the podium not giving, but receiving. You saw waves of compassion, love, concern, support, prayer, what-have-you. You saw, in my opinion, God, as we understand him, at work. And it would be wonderful if I could tell you that I left that stage that day and everything was fine. But, I didn't. I left there and it got steadily worse and I went about making plans to die.

It never once entered my mind to drink or take pills, but I had been going to doctors and they were always giving me prescriptions for tranquilizers. I'd get them filled, come home, and put them in the medicine chest. Oh, I had a beautiful selection. There were green ones and black ones and orange ones and white ones. It looked like a rainbow and I was going to find the pot at the end of the rainbow.

I revised my Will, I got rid of a lot of books and things like that that I could dispose of, and I realized that it was no longer a question in my mind of. .. *If* I was going to die, but just *how* I was going to do it. I decided that the tranquilizers would be the best route. On the morning of November 14, 1970, last year, it was

Sharing

about ten o'clock in the morning and I decided I just simply couldn't go on any longer. I couldn't face anything any longer. .. And I took a big handful of the tranquilizers and I put them in my mouth. Only God knows why I didn't swallow them. All I know is I couldn't. Whether it was Catholicism, AA, you, prayers, the prayers of people who have gone on, I don't know. All I know is I took them out of my mouth. I couldn't swallow them. And, when I had them out, looking at them in my hand, the door opened and a friend that my doctor had gotten in touch with because he had seen me the day before, walked in and he said, "Your doctor has begged me to come and take you to the hospital." And I said, "All right, I'll go. I don't think it will do me any good, but I don't want to go on living and I can't die, so I guess once again, I'll have to throw in the towel and say I would rather live than die." I went into the psychiatric ward of Mt. Sinai Hospital and I left there 26 days later, after having six shock treatments that reversed the depression and I came out knowing that I would be able to make it.

On the last day of the year, I went into escrow on the sale of the house. That, again, is another miracle. There was absolutely no loan company in that part of the state that would touch that house. The assessment on it had been doubled, the property taxes had tripled, and not one person would loan on it … not a bank, not a mortgage company, not anybody. And yet, the man that wanted to buy it came ... the one buyer that fell in love

The Rest of Your Life

with the place, finally managed to come up with enough money. I ended up taking an actual $16,000 cash equity loss on it, but he wanted it, and I wanted out. It was sold. I moved into an apartment in Encino and I've started putting my life back together again.

Now, that's the experience. But what, what do I have to share with you? I mean, it would have been awful to go through that and then now end and say, "Well, okay kids, I came through and I didn't drink, and fine and dandy. I didn't and I'm grateful to God." But now I'll try to tell you, in what time I have left here, what gets clearer in my mind every day.

In the first place, always before when I had been in AA, all these years when I'd worked with other people, when they told me about depression, I would think ... yes, I've had depression. But I never had a depression; I didn't have a depression at all. A depression, I believe, is mass anger turned in upon you. It has nothing to do at all with self-pity. Self-pity is not nearly as destructive or as dangerous ... corrosive as it is, I believe now. Because, you see, in self-pity it's always somebody else's fault. It's not yours. In a depression, a suicidal depression that I went into, it was my fault. I had done it. I paced back and forth, I couldn't eat, I couldn't sleep, and it was back and forth. McGinnis, you had it made and you blew it. You had it made and you blew it. And again, the thing that had been with me all these years from my childhood that I didn't know about was the complete and total

Sharing

inability to forgive myself. A complete and total inability to forgive myself. You see, the only reason I was able to accept alcoholism was when I found out it wasn't my fault. That it was a disease and then I could accept it.

Also I think it entails a loss, a sense of loss. That's why so many people go into depressions, suicidal depressions, when they have lost a child or a spouse or a relative. In any case, you're always losing part of yourself, something that is you ... and you see, this is what I learned. That despite all that I thought that I had accomplished, all that I had learned, God had to teach me the ultimate lesson and that was that my self-esteem, just exactly the way I had learned it in this competitive and materialistic culture of ours, my self-esteem was made up of what I had, what I possessed, what I had in the bank, what I had to show for it, the status I had achieved, my job, my sense of being somebody. And when that begins to go ... when your self-esteem is made up of money, property, prestige, and they begin to go ... then you begin to go with it. Your self-esteem, everything that you think you are, begins to go with it, and life is no longer worth living. When I lost my job at this agency, right then, I lost the prestige and the status ... but I had the money that saved my face. When that began to go, then the rest of the self-esteem went with it and life was no longer worth living. A man who had been miraculously given his life 18 years before, no longer wanted it. It's rather painful to admit, but that's

The Rest of Your Life

the way it is. What I would conjure any of you to think about is that you too are products of this culture, and we talk a lot about it. All of these years as the sobriety went by, I thought I had learned. Our society today is filled with people running around saying, "I want to know who I am, I want to know who I am, and I want to know who I am." Then when you try to introduce them to who they are, they run screaming in the other direction. But I believe the answer to who I am is very, very simple. We are all the same we. We are human beings. And as human beings, we are heir to all the strengths as well as all the weaknesses; all the faults as well as all the assets; all the virtues as well as all the vices of every other human being. What I now know is important is not who I am, but what I am. Because when the chips are down, I am what I believe. I am where my values are and what I am willing to do about it. What I believe and what I am willing to do about it.

Some months ago, I found myself on my knees, crying out into the darkness of this bleak desolation that I found myself in, a prayer that I had never uttered before in my life. It was a very simple prayer from one who is wont to make very elaborate prayers. But this one said, "Please God, please God, let me come home from the wars." As far as I know, I have never read that anywhere. It came out of a heart filled with despair and anguish and self-reproach and self-hatred. But I knew the minute I heard it

Sharing

that the key word was *home ... home*. It was coming out of a guy who had never ever, in his life, felt at home.

I remember when I was a young man and I loved to go to concerts and saved my pennies for concerts. The baritones of my day, John Charles Thomas, Nelson Eddy and people like that, were wont to sing for an encore, a corny song I loved. It was called "The Hills of Home," and it tore at my heart every time I heard it. I remember the verse that said, "... all things come home at eventide ... like birds that weary of their roaming ... and, I would hasten to your side, homing." I knew that I had never felt at home. I had never felt at home in my home. I had never felt at home in my religion. And for many years, I had not felt at home even in Alcoholics Anonymous. I remember how I had thought, how I had planned, and I said, "Someday I'll have a home, and it will be mine, and the rain will be gentle on its roof and. the wind will touch it kindly." But, you see, I had to learn that a home is not stone and mortar and roof. A home is where the heart finds rest and renewal. That's where coming home is.

I am far enough along in the journey now to be able to see that there is only one ultimate coming home, and that is the final, total, complete, surrender of self to a Power greater than myself. I'm also brave enough today to believe that there will come a day, there will be a place sometime, somewhere, someday, there will be an altar or a confessional, a mountain or a valley ...

The Rest of Your Life

probably in all likelihood .. just a plain, everyday, run-of the-mill AA meeting, where I will finally no longer pull back and say, "Oh, my God, no, no, don't ask that of me, don't take that away from me too." And when that moment comes, then I know that I will have finally come home.

In the meantime, I am more at home here than anywhere I have ever been in my life. I'm more at home here for a very simple reason ... you have never, ever asked anything of me ... therefore I have been able to give you what I could afford. What I'm trying to do tonight is to tell you that I have made a return, for as T. S. Eliot said, "There will never be any end from exploring, and the end of all our exploration will be to return to the place where we started and to see it for the first time." That is why I tell you, it took something that almost killed me to return me finally to the place where I started, to see it for the first time, and to return to you tonight and tell you that this journey has been worth everything I have been asked to pay to make it.

There are probably not more than five or six of you in this room tonight that I know by name, but you are counterparts of other faces and other hearts that I do know by name in other rooms like this, and so I know you will understand when I tell you here tonight, quite simply, that I quite literally owe you my life. I quite literally owe you my sanity ... and all I have tried to do here

Sharing

tonight is to pay you a little interest on that debt. I beg your prayers and your love and for whatever they may be worth, I give you mine.

CPSIA information can be obtained
at www.ICGtesting.com
Printed in the USA
LVHW022108300720
661978LV00014B/1149